W9-AQS-970

# AN INTRODUCTION
# TO BIOETHICS

## THOMAS A. SHANNON
## JAMES D. DIGIACOMO

Theodore Lownik Library
Illinois Benedictine College
Lisle, Illinois 60532

PAULIST PRESS
New York/Ramsey/Toronto

*174.2*
*S528*

Acknowledgment
"Levels of the Definition of Death" taken from *Death, Dying, and the Biological Revolution* by Robert M. Veatch, Copyright © Yale University Press, 1976. Used by permission of the publisher.

Copyright © 1979 by
The Missionary Society
of St. Paul the Apostle
in the State of New York

All rights reserved. No part of this book may be reproduced or transmitted in any form or by any means, electronic or mechanical, including photocopying, recording or by any information storage and retrieval system without permission in writing from the Publisher.

Library of Congress
Catalog Card Number: 79-66589

ISBN: 0-8091-2257-X

Published by Paulist Press
*Editorial Office:* 1865 Broadway, New York, N.Y. 10023
*Business Office:* 545 Island Road, Ramsey, N.J. 07446

Printed and bound in the
United States of America

# CONTENTS

PREFACE .......................................... v

1. WHAT IS BIOETHICS? ......................... 1
2. THE TECHNICAL REVOLUTION ............... 9
3. ETHICAL CONCEPTS ......................... 19
4. ABORTION ..................................... 33
5. DEFINITION OF DEATH ...................... 47
6. EUTHANASIA ................................. 59
7. THE LIVING WILL .......................... 69
8. NEWBORNS WITH BIRTH DEFECTS .......... 79
9. ORGAN TRANSPLANTS ....................... 95
10. RESEARCH INVOLVING HUMAN SUBJECTS .. 105
11. BEHAVIOR MODIFICATION ................... 115
12. GENETIC ENGINEERING .................... 127
13. PATIENTS' RIGHTS ......................... 145

*To Jerry and Theresa
with gratitude*

# PREFACE

The purpose of this book is to provide an introduction to selected problems and issues in the area of bioethics as well as an overview of the basic medical problems and ethical dilemmas in that field. It is written for a lay audience which seeks to be informed about many of the developments in medicine, science and technology that have an ever increasing impact on how we live and die. Rather than developing specific arguments for particular solutions, the book indicates the basic range of problems and solutions. In this way we have provided full introduction to the issues.

Case material, discussion questions and bibliography lend the book to a variety of purposes and uses. The most basic purpose is to inform individuals of these problems and to contribute, even in a small way, to helping them assume their proper responsibility in bioethical decision-making.

Thomas A. Shannon
Associate Professor of Social Ethics
Department of Humanities
Worcester Polytechnic Institute

*Chapter One*

---

# WHAT IS BIOETHICS?

In the last third of the twentieth century, technological advances in the areas of science, medicine, and health care have given rise to a new field called bioethics. As we increase our ability to influence the length and quality of our lives by such means as organ transplants, abortion, genetic engineering, and life-support machines, we find ourselves facing ethical dilemmas which touch the very heart of the meaning and significance of human life.

The word "bioethics" means, literally, the ethics of life. That takes in a lot of territory. One of its most problematic and interesting features is its interdisciplinary character. Most of those who work in this area are convinced that no one discipline has within itself the total resources needed to deal with all the problems involved. Hence specialization is not the answer. Rather, several disciplines and professions need to cooperate, pooling their skills and resources, if we are to analyze and evaluate the political, social, economic, and value issues inherent in these fields.

## BIOETHICS

Let's look first at the "bio" part of the word. We will be studying problems which arise from several specific disciplines—e.g., the life sciences, psychology, biomedical engineering, and genetics. If we are to comprehend the issues even on an introductory level, we must examine a broad range of data from the physical and natural sciences. We will have to evaluate new procedures, policies, and applications of techniques that may be experimental or controversial. The "bio" part of bioethics demands that we take seriously both the disciplines themselves and the implications of scientific knowledge so that we may understand the issues, perceive what is at stake, and learn to evaluate possible consequences of discoveries and their application.

## BIOETHICS

The "ethics" part of bioethics must be taken with equal seriousness. When someone mentions ethics in connection with science and medicine probably one of the biggest fears that many people have is that the function of ethics is to act as a big, nasty police officer who always seems to say, "You can't do that; it's unethical." And of course that does happen. People do have convictions, and we live in a society in which we have the freedom to speak out. Also, there are many who conceive of ethics in a very narrow sense and try to establish standards which must be followed by all. We have all seen repression perpetrated in the name of morality and religion. On the other hand, ethics is basically an evaluation of various claims or affirmations of rights, so that we may order our lives in accordance with them. It is an attempt to determine the fundamental values by which we live. When seen in a social context, it is an attempt to evaluate my actions and the actions of others according to a methodology or according to certain basic values.

This attempt may take one of two basic forms—rule ethics or act ethics. Rule ethics appeals to a set of criteria, norms, principles, or rules to determine what is the right or ethical thing to do. Act ethics, on the other hand, judges rightness or wrongness by looking to the meaning or consequences of the act itself.

A form of rule ethics with which we are all familiar comes from our Judaeo-Christian heritage: the Ten Commandments. These are simple rules stating what one should not do: one should not lie, kill, commit adultery, steal, etc. By appealing to the rule, a person determines what may or may not be done. A more sophisticated type of rule ethics is the system of natural law. According to this theory, nature has an order or structure that can be discovered by human reason, and correct or ethical conduct consists in conforming one's action to this order of nature.

An example of act ethics is utilitarianism. According to this theory, an act is ethical when it promotes the greatest amount of good for the greatest number of people. Another type is situation ethics or contextualism, in which we determine what is ethical by looking not to a rule but to the consequences or the meaning of the situation.

Samuel Gorovitz calls bioethics the "critical examination of the moral dimensions of decision-making in health-related contexts and in contexts involving the biological sciences."[1] If you look closely at this definition you can see that bioethics, rather than being a self-contained discipline, is the application of traditional ethical theory to a specific area such as science, medicine, or health care in general. Thus physicians and other scientists do not have a unique code of ethics proper to them; they are bound by common ethical principles that apply to

---

[1]Samuel Gorovitz, "Bioethics and Social Responsibility," *The Monist* 60:3 (January 1977).

everyone. What is unique about bioethics is not its methodology but its subject matter. It works in an area that is common to many disciplines and thus deals with problems that may be unique. But that does not mean that its methods or orientation constitute a new discipline.

The list of problems with which bioethics deals makes up the table of contents of this book. It includes, among others, such specific topics as abortion, the definition of death, euthanasia, birth defects, genetic engineering, organ transplants, experiments on human subjects, behavior modification, and patients' rights. Related problems include the regulation of health care, responsibility for dependent persons, patient-doctor relationships, and the scope of medical practice. When we try to deal with these, certain values come to the fore to be examined and discussed. And we realize that we need a certain amount of empirical data so that our statement of the problems as well as our proposed solutions may be based on accurate factual information and analysis.

In the course of this book, certain themes will recur from time to time. We will find ourselves asking: What is normal? What is natural? What does it mean to be free? What are the scope and limits of responsibility? Traditional ethical concepts like rights, duties, justice, and personhood will play a large role in our attempts to understand the critical issues at stake. The way we define these concepts and issues will determine, to a great extent, the way we resolve the dilemmas that confront us at every turn. Thus it is important to be aware of the basic meaning of these terms that are so often used and so seldom clearly understood.

Therefore bioethics takes on a broad range of problems that arise from science in general and medicine in particular. It tries to uncover and clarify the value dilemmas that are brought on by technological breakthroughs in science and medicine and even in ordinary medical practice. Bioethics is everybody's business, because it makes us attend to problems that all of us must eventually face. By examining these problems in at least an introductory way, this book may help you to assume more responsibility for your own destiny and eventually to take an active part in setting policies which will touch the lives of more and more people as time goes on.

But before we begin, it is wise to take a backward glance at the events that have brought us to this critical juncture in the history of science and medicine. What are the discoveries and the inventions that have, in the last decade, forced us to confront our responsibilities in new and unfamiliar ways? It is time to look at one of the big stories of the late twentieth century: the technical revolution.

## TOPICS FOR DISCUSSION

1. Why is bioethics considered an interdisciplinary field?

2. "Bioethics is everybody's business, because it makes us attend to problems that all of us must eventually face." Do you have any data from personal experience or observation that would support this statement?

3. What are some of the ways in which bioethical issues and concerns have made headlines in the past few years?

## RESOURCES

Beauchamp, Tom L., and LeRoy Walters, editors. *Contemporary Issues in Bioethics.* Encino, California: Dickinson Publishing Company, 1978.

Brody, Howard, *Ethical Decisions in Medicine.* Boston: Little, Brown and Company, 1976.

Fletcher, Joseph. *Morals and Medicine.* Boston: Beacon Press, 1954.

Gorovitz, Samuel, *et al.*, editors. *Moral Problems in Medicine.* Englewood Cliffs, New Jersey: Prentice-Hall, 1976.

Haring, Bernard, *Medical Ethics.* Notre Dame, Indiana: Fides Publishers, 1973.

Hunt, Robert, and John Arras, editors. *Ethical Issues in Modern Medicine.* Palo Alto, California: Mayfield Publishing Company, 1977.

Jakobovitz, Immanuel. *Jewish Medical Ethics.* New York: Block Publishing Company, 1959.

Kelly, Gerald. *Medico-Moral Problems.* St. Louis: Catholic Hospital Association, 1958.

Nelson, James B. *Human Medicine: Ethical Perspectives on New Medical Issues.* Minneapolis: Augsburg Publishing House, 1973.

Ramsey, Paul. *The Patient as Person.* New Haven: Yale University Press, 1970.

————*Ethics at the Edges of Life: Medical and Legal Intersections.* New Haven: Yale University Press, 1978.

Reiser, Stanley J., Arthur J. Dyck, and William J. Curran, editors. *Ethics in Medicine: Historical Perspectives and Contemporary Concerns.* Cambridge: The MIT Press, 1977.

Shannon, Thomas A., editor. *Bioethics.* New York: Paulist Press, 1976.

Veatch, Robert M. *Case Studies in Medical Ethics.* Cambridge: Harvard University Press, 1977.

Of general interest and importance in the field of bioethics is the recently published *Encylopedia of Bioethics* (New York: The Free Press, 1978). This is a basic reference work of all the major topics in bioethics. Each entry also contains additional bibliography.

*Hospital.* BNW 16 mm. 84 minutes. Rent: $100. Sale: $750. Distributor: Zipporah Films, 54 Lewis Wharf, Boston, Mass. 02110.

*Chapter Two*

---

# THE TECHNICAL REVOLUTION

The technical revolution began a long time ago with the rise of modern science and the Industrial Revolution, accelerated dramatically during the twentieth century, and recently received its greatest impetus from the development of nuclear energy. There is no area of our life that is not touched by technology. Contraception and the technique of amniocentesis help determine whether and when and how we begin life; cyrogenics offers the hope of eliminating death by freezing the dead until a cure for their sickness can be found. And between the beginning and end of life, technology has an impact on almost everything we do, from the way we eat to the way we live, from the way we work to the way we play.

Some see this as a blessing, because the quality of life has markedly improved. Others see it as a curse and blame it for polluting our environment and depleting our resources. And still others recognize both the benefits and the problems and pronounce it a mixed blessing. In any event, it is obvious that life as we know it in the late twentieth century has been dramatically changed by the application of scientific discoveries to our daily lives.

## THE ROOTS OF TECHNOLOGY

Where did the technological society come from? The process has been long and complex, but we can now distinguish several important elements that combined to produce it:[1]

• *The empirical or pragmatic spirit.* This is one of the most significant and distinctive contributions of American culture. The emphasis is on getting the job done. The important question is not whether we want or need a new device, but whether it will work.

• *Functionalism.* Closely connected with the pragmatic spirit is the stress on performance. How does an individual or a technology perform? Again, the important question is not *why* but *how.*

• *Preoccupation with means, not ends.* The stress is on process rather than purpose. It is usually easier to figure out *how* something can be done than to agree on *what* should be done. So technical strategies or solutions are easily accepted, because we tend uncritically to assume that if we have solved the problem of the means, then we have also solved the problem of the end.

• *Preference for quantity over quality.* It is a common human tendency to choose *more* rather than *better.* This is supported by the standard we use to measure the growth of our nation—the gross national product. Our standard of living has been dramatically improved by the increased availability of consumer goods. And since improvements in production are promoted by technological developments, it seems preferable to continue in this direction.

• *The link between efficiency and profit.* When we use

---

[1]Norman J. Faramelli, *Technethics*, New York: Friendship Press, 1971. pp. 31ff.

rational industrial systems in production, we can turn out items in greater numbers. And if the product is less labor intensive, it may be possible to increase profits dramatically. And of course profits are important in measuring the health of the country. Thus we have another reason to choose means over ends.

• *The move to manipulation.* The rational control of natural processes is becoming an extremely important feature of our social life. This is quite clear when we review our industrial history. Our society has increasingly valued the ability to control and direct processes in accord with the ends we choose. This has created a more highly controlled system which permits a greater increase in the gross national product. If we look at recent developments in genetics, we will see the same forces at work—only now, instead of controlling the processes that produce things, we attempt to control the processes that produce people.

## WHAT IS TECHNOLOGY?

Knowing what has led to technology, however, does not tell us what it is. Various definitions have been offered and deserve our consideration. For some, technology is just a name for the hardware used in certain processes, such as computers, assembly lines, and machines of all kinds. This is at least an important dimension of technology, since it is obvious that such hardware has significantly changed our life-style and influenced our standard of living. But others like Jacques Ellul[2] define technology as more than hardware and prefer to use the broader concept of technique. This is a complex of standardized means for attaining a pre-determined result not through spontaneous and unreflexive behavior but by a deliberate and rationalized process. The emphasis here is not on

[2]Jacques Ellul, *The Technological Society*, New York: Vintage Books, 1964, pp. 13ff.

machines or hardware but on the process by which behavior is organized according to a rational plan.

Ellul's approach gives us a broader perspective on technology and how it works. It describes not only an industrial methodology but a social and cultural phenomenon. In its widest meaning, technology is simply applied knowledge, or the application of organized knowledge for achieving specific, practical purposes. This kind of definition incorporates not only the mechanical or hardware dimension of technology but also its planning and organizational features. It delineates an overarching social reality that affects our society, way of life, and standard of living not only in obvious, dramatic ways but also in ways that are subtle and unperceived at the present time.

Daniel Bell's analysis[3] of technology distinguished five essential dimensions: function, energy, fabrication, communication and control, and regulated decision-making.

• *Function.* When designing a product, the technological mentality does not take nature for a guide unless nature is efficient. A product is shaped by its function, and the important thing is *how* something functions, not the purpose for which the function is designed.

• *Energy.* In a technological society, natural sources of power like water, wind, and personal strength are replaced with created, artificial sources such as coal and oil. Now that these are in short supply, new sources of energy such as nuclear power are being developed. Natural sources are considered inadequate to sustain the level of energy needed to run any of the individual segments of our society, so we have to go beyond the traditional ways of seeking power.

• *Fabrication.* This is the word Bell uses to describe the knowledge that produces standardization, a way of doing things in a reproducible manner through the action of inter-

---

[3]Daniel Bell, Faculty Seminar Presentation, Worcester Polytechnic Institute, 1976. Cf. also: *The Coming of the Post-Industrial Society*, New York: Basic Books, 1975.

changeable parts. This is extremely important not only in mass production but also in other areas such as the organization of large corporations and even education. The emphasis is on training large numbers of people in the most efficient manner possible so that the organization runs smoothly.

• *Communication and control.* These are concerned with the extension and centralization of power. This is because the system needs information so that it can perpetuate itself and function smoothly. Then there is a strong tendency for power to be centralized around the sources of information and around the individuals who control the flow of information. Visitors from outer space, if they are smart, will tell the first earthling they meet, "Take me to your computer."

• *Decision-making rules.* In a system where function, fabrication and communication play vital roles, it is extremely important to have set procedures for exchanging information and making decisions. Decision-making can no longer be left to random processes, or the entire system will break down. The process must be quick and efficient and conducted according to specific rules so that the parts of the system may work harmoniously—and this necessarily calls for even greater centralization of power.

## IMPACT ON CULTURE

When we consider these different aspects of technology and remember that we are dealing with knowledge that is not theoretical but applied, we can begin to understand the impact that it has had on our culture. Machines change our basic self-perception and enable us to define ourselves in ways that we thought impossible in the past. We can achieve more in less time than we thought possible a mere twenty-five years ago. We can increase our life-span and make interventions in nature that were inconceivable only several generations ago. We have the potential for literally redesigning our own future.

On the other hand, we are experiencing severe problems as a result of these new powers. Our need for ever increasing amounts of power has blinded us to the fact that our energy sources are finite, and now our reserves are simply running out. Hence we are now engaged in a frantic search to develop an energy policy and to find alternate sources of energy. From a medical perspective, we have the ability to prolong life almost indefinitely. Yet we find it increasingly difficult to define what a human being is, whether a human being is alive or dead, and whether we should or should not prolong a person's life. We also have a standard of living that is higher and have more consumer goods available than anywhere else in the world. Yet such opportunities do not seem to bring as much personal satisfaction as was expected. A nagging sense of disillusionment has followed in the wake of the advances made by our technological society. There is a feeling abroad that more is not always better, and that we have taken a wrong turn somewhere but are unable to retrace our steps.

Because of the variety of effects that technology has had on humans and human society, many people are suggesting that it must be evaluated both to predict and to prevent undesirable consequences and to plan specifically for outcomes that are perceived as valuable. One way of doing this is through the newly developed methodology of technology assessment. This is the systematic study of the effects on society that may occur when a technology is introduced, expanded, or modified, with special emphasis on the impacts that are unintended, indirect, and delayed.[4] It attempts to evaluate a broad range of effects: environmental, social, economic, and political. It is necessary to evaluate such effects because of the consequent impact they may have on society.

Technology assessment is obviously not foolproof. It is subject to the limitations of our present state of knowledge and our ability to ask the right questions. However, it does move us a step ahead by at least raising the problem of the consequences that follow on the uninhibited application of

---

[4]LeRoy Walters, "Technology Assessments and Genetics," *Theological Studies* 33:666 (December 1972).

technology. By evaluating these in advance, we may be able to make decisions that minimize the damage and maximize the benefits.

Technology is here to stay. It is a significant and essential part of our contemporary social structure that has brought us many benefits. By raising the quality of life, it has made it possible for us to take significant steps beyond what even our parents dreamed of. However, it has also raised many problems, and it is to one specific dimension of these problems, the medical, that we will be turning in the rest of this book.

## TOPICS FOR DISCUSSION

1. America is preeminently a pragmatic, practical, "can-do" society. Broadly speaking, what are the *strengths* and the *weaknesses* inherent in such a model?

2. Can you think of an example from any familiar area of daily life where *more* has not been *better*?

3. Give an example of undesirable second order consequences—indirect and unintended effects of the application of a technology. Could the bad side-effects have been foreseen or avoided?

4. Look at your daily routine. What are some of the ways that technology *enriches* your life? Do you see any ways in which it *impoverishes* you?

## RESOURCES

Barbour, Ian G., editor. *Science and Religion*. New York: Harper and Row, 1968.

Bell, Daniel. *The Coming of the Post-Industrial Society*. New York: Basic Books, 1973.

Bronowsky, Jacob. *Science and Human Values*. New York: Harper and Row, 1965.

Callahan, Daniel. *The Tyranny of Survival*. New York: Macmillan, 1973.

Ellul, Jacques. *The Technological Society*. New York: Vintage Books, 1964.

Ferkiss, Victor C. *The Future of Technological Civilization.* New York: George Braziller, 1974.

——*Technological Man: The Myth and the Reality.* New York: George Braziller, 1969.

Heilbroner, Robert L. *An Inquiry into the Human Prospect.* New York: W. W. Norton and Company, 1974.

Kuhn, Thomas S. *The Structure of the Scientific Revolutions.* Second Edition. Chicago: University of Chicago Press, 1970.

Ravetz, Jerome. *Scientific Knowledge and Social Problems.* New York: Oxford University Press, 1971.

*Projection 70's Medicine.* Color. 16 mm. 25 minutes. Rent: $25. Distributor: American Educational Films, 132 Lasky Dr., Beverly Hills, Calif. 90212.

*Chapter Three*

---

# ETHICAL CONCEPTS

In order to deal effectively with the moral dimensions of medical problems arising from technology, we need a grasp of certain basic ethical concepts. These will be coming up from time to time in the course of this book, so this is a good time to define them as clearly as we can. This chapter will not offer a comprehensive discussion of these ideas, but it will give their essential elements which will serve as a background for topics that will be discussed later.

Six fundamental concepts occur often enough in discussions of bioethics to merit extended discussion beforehand. They are: (1) the sanctity of human life; (2) the principle of double effect; (3) the principle of totality; (4) ordinary and extraordinary treatment; (5) justice; (6) the role of the Church. Let us now consider each of these in some detail.

## THE SANCTITY OF HUMAN LIFE
This is perhaps the most fundamental consideration in bioethical discussions, for if human life is not sacred, then

little else is. We experience it as something valuable and worthy of respect; hence any intervention or interference in human life must be evaluated and tested by reference to this central issue.

Why is human life sacred? In some ways this question is easy to answer, in some ways difficult. On the one hand, our general experience of it as something good and worthwhile helps us perceive it as deserving to be preserved and shared. On the other hand, the dignity of human life is a foundational concept grounded primarily in itself and must be supported by its own self-evident quality. This makes it hard to come up with a definition acceptable to everyone, since we do not all experience life in the same way or give it the same rank in our scale of values. The issue of human dignity becomes particularly acute at the beginning and at the end of life. When does life begin and become worthy of respect? When is it finished and no longer to be esteemed? Thus the primary problem with the concept of the sanctity or dignity of human life is not precisely one of definition or experience of worth, but rather of applying that definition. This gives rise to some of the ongoing dilemmas in bioethics which will be discussed later.

What are the sources of this value? One lies within human experience itself. Human life is perceived as sacred or having a certain dignity because human beings are basically valuable individuals. "People are important." As seen within the philosophy called humanism, the dignity of human existence rises from within itself, from within its own meaning, and has as its purpose and justification nothing other than itself. Similar and complementary to this point of view is a theological perspective which suggests that human dignity receives its sanctity from being created by God. Because individuals are made in the image and likeness of God, they are worthy of respect and receive the dignity that comes from being a special part of creation. These two perceptions, the philosophical and the theological, can be used separately or in combination in a variety of arguments. Again, the problem comes not in grounding but in applying the concept.

Daniel Callahan has identified five elements which he considers critical to the concept of the sanctity of human life.[1] The first of these is the survival of the human species. It is good that humans exist, and they ought to work toward survival and act in ways that make a viable future possible for others. A second element is the preservation of family lines. People should be free to propagate their own children and to determine their family size. A third important element is the right of human beings to enjoy the protection of their fellow human beings. People do not have the right unjustly to deprive others of life or to create social, economic, medical, or political conditions which would have the effect of destroying or devaluing life. The fourth element is respect for personal choice and self-determination, which would also include mental and emotional integrity. By this Callahan means that persons should be allowed to make for themselves those choices which affect their personal fates. They have, in other words, the right to determine their own lives and to be themselves. The final element is personal bodily inviolability. My body, with its organs, is my own; indeed, it is my*self*. Thus no one should violate or impose upon my body or any part of it, without my permission.

These dimensions of the sanctity of life are not all-inclusive, but they do flesh out the concept and give us an orientation that will be helpful in resolving several problems within bioethics.

## THE PRINCIPLE OF DOUBLE EFFECT

A troublesome situation that occurs again and again in medical practice is one in which a proposed action will produce two effects, one good and the other bad. The first result is legitimate, and the one we want to achieve; the second is evil and not the one we intend, but is inseparable from the first. The agonizing question arises: May we seek the good and tolerate the evil? To deal with these dilemmas, the principle of

---

[1]Daniel Callahan. *Abortion: Law, Choice and Morality*, New York: Macmillan, 1972, pp. 307ff.

double effect has been formulated. It permits us to perform the good act that has evil consequences, so long as the following conditions are fulfilled:

1. The action, in and of itself, must not be evil. This simply reaffirms the fundamental moral principle that we may never do evil. Just because the act may also have some good consequences does not thereby make it justified.

2. The evil may not be the means of producing the good effect. Again, this is a restatement of a traditional moral principle: the end does not justify the means. We are forbidden to rob banks, even if we just want the money to get a better education for our children. The end or purpose is good, but the means of obtaining it is wrong.

3. The evil effect is not intended, but merely permitted or tolerated. What this means is that our primary intention is to achieve the good effect. We may foresee the undesirable effects, but we do not *seek* them; we only permit them. The distinction is subtle, and may seem to some merely verbal, but it is important. This dimension of the principle is saying that we may perform what is good, even though some unfortunate consequence may coincide with or follow from our doing of good.

4. There must be a proportionate reason for performing the action in spite of the consequences it has. When placed in the balance, the good should outweigh the bad. This balancing of effects and values opens up a broad range of problems and dilemmas for those in ethics generally and in bioethics particularly. Sometimes the evaluation of the proportionality of effects is very complicated, but it must be done if we are to proceed with integrity.

Richard McCormick suggests that proportionality or proportionate reason involves three elements.[2] First, there is at stake a value at least equal in importance to the one sacrificed. In other words, something extremely important is being

---

[2]Richard McCormick, S.J., *Ambiguity and Moral Choice*, Department of Theology, Marquette University, p. 93.

done, and the good intended is at least equal to the evil that may follow in its wake. Second, there is no less harmful way, here and now, of protecting the value we espouse. In order to act responsibly in some complex moral situations, we may have to make some trade-offs to achieve a particular good, but in doing so we must take care to produce the least possible harm. Third, the way a value is protected here and now should not undermine that value in the future. We are sometimes tempted to cut corners in order to achieve a particular solution to a pressing problem, but the long-range effect may be the opening up of a host of problems that would eventually undermine the very ground on which we stand.

McCormick is making an important point: that achieving a sense of proportionality is not a kind of mental calculus that merely adds up goods and evils. Rather, it is an attempt to achieve a certain order of goods by which we can evaluate actions that will have a broad range of consequences. This is not an easy task, and it involves more than arithmetic. It is a way of examining my life, my values, and my intentions. The principle of double effect provides a way to analyze ambiguous situations, but it does not remove the ambiguity, and it does not remove our obligation of a profound search of conscience which must necessarily precede the taking of action.

## THE PRINCIPLE OF TOTALITY

The principle of totality, a traditional element in bioethical discussions, states simply that a part exists for the sake of the whole. It applies primarily to amputations and to the removal of diseased organs, but is also a summary way of stating other concerns in ethics. The first is that persons are not the owners but the administrators of their bodies. Second, an individual may dispose of bodily members or functions only insofar as this is medically required. This is done when it is necessary for the good of one's being as a whole, to ensure one's existence, or to remove some damage which cannot be avoided or repaired. Thus the principle of totality is a way of affirming that we may legitimately sacrifice a part of the body if this is necessary to preserve the health of the entire body.

## ORDINARY AND EXTRAORDINARY TREATMENT

The distinction between ordinary and extraordinary means of treatment is an important and helpful consideration in making difficult medical decisions. Generally speaking, ordinary means of preserving life are all medicines, treatments, and operations which offer a reasonable amount of benefit for the patient and which can be obtained and used without excessive expense, pain, or other inconveniences. On the other hand, extraordinary means are those medicines, treatments, and operations which cannot be obtained or used without excessive expense, pain, or inconvenience, or which, if used, would not offer a reasonable hope of benefit.[3]

It is important to remember that these are ethical, not medical definitions. Such distinctions are made with difficulty in ethics, but are even harder in medical practice. The rate of medical progress makes this year's extraordinary treatment next year's ordinary procedure. On the other hand, a procedure such as heart surgery may be extremely expensive, painful, and inconvenient for the patient, but still be the standard means of treating this particular ailment. One then has to ask whether such standard medical treatment is ordinary or extraordinary from an ethical perspective. As far as medicine is concerned, what is ordinary is the standard or recognized treatment for a particular illness or what is ordinarily expected in treating a particular problem. This does not make it any easier to say what is ordinary and extraordinary in ethical terms, but it does provide a framework for such evaluation.

Then, too, there is something we must not forget about the medical profession. Its whole thrust is to cure, to restore health, to preserve life. Members of the medical profession tend to want to do everything possible to cure every illness;

[3]Gerald Kelly, S.J., *Medical-Moral Problems*, St. Louis: The Catholic Hospital Association, 1958, p. 129.

they have a deep-seated resistance to doing anything that may kill or shorten life. Theirs is a calling to conquer death and to eradicate illness, and any effort short of that may be seen as a surrender to the enemy. Many of them share a strong cultural bias that science can do everything. This implies that in fighting illness, whatever *can* be done *ought* to be done, regardless of the effects that such treatment may or may not have on the illness or the patient.

On the other hand, countering these professional attitudes and values, there is the ethical principle which affirms that one is not bound to use extraordinary means to preserve life. Underlying this principle is the conviction that physical life, while very important, is not the highest value. In the Christian tradition, for example, it is outranked by one's eternal destiny. Human experience tells us that all people die; must we, therefore, do everything possible to postpone the end? At some point in the progression of a serious disease, further treatment may be useless in terms of effecting a cure. Therefore this tradition recognizes limits to what we must do in trying to cure sickness or preserve life. While this distinction does not produce any hard and fast rule about what to do in a particular situation, it does take into account certain truths we might otherwise lose sight of: that medicine and science have limits, and that people eventually die. At this point Paul Ramsey reminds us that while there are limits to our attempts to cure, we should never stop caring for the person who is sick or dying.[4]

## JUSTICE

Another critical concept in bioethics is that of justice. This is the virtue which attempts to give to a person what is owed or due, so that the person receives what is deserved and what has been legitimately claimed. Justice demands that similar cases be treated in similar fashion, and dissimilar

[4]Paul Ramsey, *The Patient as Person*, New Haven: Yale University Press, 1970, pp. 113ff.

cases in dissimilar fashion. To put it in a different way: equals should be treated equally and unequals unequally.

There are three kinds of justice. *Commutative* justice calls for fairness in various types of exchanges such as wages and prices. *Retributive* justice demands that one pay back what is due. It exacts punishment for breaking a law and obliges the offender to return what has been stolen. *Distributive* justice regulates the sharing of social benefits and burdens, and it is this aspect that is most critical for bioethics.

The reason why distributive justice is so important is that the problem of allocation of resources cuts across many of the specific issues in bioethics. At least four different norms of distribution are possible. The first seeks strict *equality*: divide the amount of resources by the number of people, and give each one an equal share, regardless of other circumstances. The second would distribute resources according to *need*. Some would receive a lot, others would receive a little of the item in question. This would be determined and justified on the basis of the particular need of an individual. A third formula would regulate allocation according to individual *effort*. The harder one tries to reach a certain goal, the more he or she receives. Finally, the norm of distribution can be *social contribution*. Those who have given the most to society would receive the most in return; those who have given little would receive little. Each of these methods of distribution has its own strengths and weaknesses. What is important is to recognize the strong and weak points of each and also their implications.

## THE ROLE OF THE CHURCH

A final important element in decision-making, especially in Roman Catholic bioethics, is the role of the Church. This raises many problems which have extremely complicated backgrounds and are open to different interpretations. The Church's teachings on specific topics have given rise to much debate; still, it has a tradition of systematic reflection on moral issues and has accumulated a certain amount of experience in this field. Two extreme reactions should be avoided.

The first would simply dismiss the Church as irrelevant; the second would accept its teachings without question. An open, critical attitude would be preferable. This would re-evaluate many of the Church's specific solutions in the light of current developments in research and medicine and would deal with the intrinsic merits of the arguments put forth by Church authorities in support of positions taken.

When you try to give the proper place to Church teaching in ethical questions, you must clarify the relationship between revelation and natural law. The magisterium of the Church claims to be the guardian and interpreter of natural law, and it bases this claim on the New Testament and the teachings of Jesus. However, this claim has never been specified other than on the general ground of the Church's having authority to teach. There seems to be no precise teaching in the New Testament on the nature or structure of the Church, let alone on how the Church might relate to a particular theory of moral philosophy. The problem here is that the Church is claiming a privileged position in a philosophical argument. Such a claim may in fact weaken an argument, especially if the argument happens to be poorly developed. Revelation is not a fail-safe mechanism for poor reasoning or weak philosophical analysis. To make it serve such an unworthy purpose cheapens revelation and erodes the integrity of the Church.

A second issue is the function of Church authority itself. It is unfortunate that this authority has been seriously weakened in the past few decades, for obedience to authority within a religious community is still a meaningful virtue. On the other hand, obedience is neither the only nor the highest virtue. Authority and the commands it gives must be continually evaluated and tested, and we must be careful not to reduce the proper exercise of authority to mere social control. Just because a particular practice may ensure good order, that does not make it right. The ethical significance of the practice must be judged on its own merits, without primary reference to the control of individual actions.

It is also extremely important to remember that Church

authorities have never issued any infallible declarations on issues of morals. Various actions and practices have been absolutely prohibited, but there has been no infallible statement on their inherent morality. The implication is that declarations of the magisterium on moral issues are subject to re-evaluation. This does not mean, of course, that such declarations are meaningless, useless, or irrational. It simply means that they are not necessarily the final word on the subject, and that it is possible for the community to re-examine, reinterpret, and reapply these statements in contemporary situations.

Finally, the relation between revelation and philosophy must be worked out. Both embody values that are important for ethical reflection. Revelation and philosophy are not necessarily opposed, but neither are they automatically in harmony. They are best viewed as standing in a dialectical relationship, so that each may be tested and may contribute to the solution of critical human problems. Such a dialectic ensures the formation of a mature conscience, sensitive to the reality of God and to the meaning of the human situation.

This chapter has not provided an all-inclusive list of concepts and principles operative in bioethical analysis. It is more of an opening statement which we hope will alert the reader to some of the primary concerns in this field. It should also serve as an introductory framework for some of the concepts that will be developed later, as we address ourselves to some of the most pressing and frequently experienced ethical dilemmas arising from developments in science, medicine, and technology.

## TOPICS FOR DISCUSSION

1. Why is it difficult to "prove" that life is sacred?

2. Do you think that everyone agrees that human beings are precious and valuable in themselves, regardless of their talents and accomplishments?

3. Secular humanism and the Judaeo-Christian tradition

agree on the value and worth of human life. How do their points of view differ?

4. Why do medical professionals find it hard to place limits on their struggle against disease and death?

5. To some people, the principle of double effect sounds like "the end justifies the means." Explain the difference.

6. The authors say that extremes should be avoided in reacting to authoritative Church statements in the moral sphere. What are those extremes? What do they mean by an "open, critical attitude toward Church teachings"?

## RESOURCES

Appel, Gerison. *A Philosophy of Mizvot: The Religious-Ethical Concepts of Judaism, Their Roots in Biblical Law and the Oral Tradition.* New York: KTAV Publishing House, 1975.

Ashley, Benedict M., O. P. and Kevin D. O'Rourke, O. P. *Health Care Ethics: A Theological Analysis.* St. Louis: The Catholic Hospital Association, 1978.

Bayles, Michael D., editor. *Contemporary Utilitarianism.* New York: Doubleday, 1968.

DeGeorge, Richard T., editor. *Ethics and Society: Original Essays on Contemporary Moral Problems.* New York: Doubleday, 1966.

Dworkin, Ronald. *Taking Rights Seriously.* Cambridge: Harvard University Press, 1977.

Dyck, Arthur J. *On Human Care: An Introduction to Ethics.* Nashville: Abingdon Press, 1977.

Fried, Charles. *An Anatomy of Values: Problems of Personal and Social Choice.* Cambridge: Harvard University Press, 1970.

Gustafson, James M. *Protestant and Roman Catholic Ethics.* Chicago: University of Chicago Press, 1978.

MacIntyre, Alistair. *A Short History of Ethics.* New York: Macmillan, 1966.

Maguire, Daniel C. *The Moral Choice.* Garden City, New York: Doubleday, 1978.

Nozick, Robert. *Anarchy, State and Utopia*. New York: Basic Books, 1974.

Ramsey, Paul. *Deeds and Rules in Christian Ethics*. New York: Charles Scribner's Sons, 1967.

Rawls, John. *A Theory of Justice*. Cambridge: Harvard University Press, 1971.

Taylor, Paul W., editor. *Principles of Ethics: An Introduction*. Encino, California: Dickinson Publishing Company, 1975.

*Chapter Four*

---

# ABORTION

When Evelyn told her husband John that she was pregnant, they faced the most serious crisis of their twelve-year marriage. Through careful planning, they had limited their family to two children, aged ten and eight. He was a bank teller, and she had been a high school teacher for the past six years. To enable her to pursue her career, they had been using a contraceptive and had shared equally in household responsibilities. The new baby would cause financial problems, but John felt they could handle them, and he was willing to continue helping with household chores. It came as a shock to him when Evelyn declared that she wanted an abortion.

Because of the Supreme Court decision, the abortion would be legal and since it would be performed in the first trimester, John could not prohibit it. But John considered it abhorrent to abort a child of his. According to the law, Evelyn's freedom "to control her own body" was decisive, but now not only her body but her career, her peace of mind, and the welfare of her children were at stake. Although John could not legally prevent Evelyn from extinguishing a life he had helped create, he pointed out to her that since he was equally responsible for the child's conception and would share equally in its care, he should also share equally in the decision.

Theirs was a strong marriage, so Evelyn agreed that they could not make the decision on purely legalistic grounds. They knew that abortion in their case was legal, but they were not sure it was right. They would have to work out the problem together.

These two people were dealing on a personal level with one of the most divisive and politically sensitive questions of our time. Ever since the Supreme Court's 1973 decision made abortion legal for women in Evelyn's position, Americans have been taking sides. Patterns of marriage and family life have been changed, national movements have been mobilized, and political careers have been made and destroyed, depending on people's perception of this moral issue. In order to clarify the ethical problems and choices involved, we should begin by discussing three critical court decisions of the seventies.

## LANDMARK DECISIONS

The first case is that of *Roe v. Wade*,[1] decided on January 22, 1973. This first major Supreme Court decision on abortion was handed down in a class action suit challenging the constitutionality of Texas laws which made it a crime to procure or attempt an abortion except on medical advice for the purpose of saving the mother's life. In ruling that these laws were unconstitutional, it in effect struck down all similar laws in other states. The primary argument made by the Court was that the right of privacy was broad enough to include a woman's decision to terminate her pregnancy. Also included in this decision was the declaration that the fetus is not a person in the constitutional sense.

[1] 410 U.S. 113.

# THE SUPREME COURT AND ABORTION

| Case | Decision | Other Effects |
|------|----------|---------------|
| Roe v. Wade (1973) | Declared unconstitutional a Texas law forbidding abortion except to save mother's life | In effect, declared similar laws in other states unconstitutional<br>Gave decision to abort in first trimester to woman and physician<br>Gave state power to regulate abortion in second trimester for reasons related to maternal health<br>Gave state power to regulate and even forbid abortion in third trimester, except to preserve mother's life |
| Planned Parenthood of Central Missouri v. Danforth (1976) | Struck down two requirements of Missouri abortion law | Husband's consent not required for first trimester abortion<br>Consent of parent or guardian not required for abortion on woman who is unmarried or under 18 years of age. |
| Beal v. Doe (1977) | Declared that states participating in the Medicaid program are not required to fund non-therapeutic abortions | Abortions in Medicaid states may be dependent on financial considerations |

Three findings in this case looked to each of the three-month periods of a normal pregnancy. 1. During the first trimester, the decision of whether or not to abort is left to the medical judgment of the pregnant woman and her physician. Evelyn qualified under this heading, since she was only five weeks pregnant. 2. For a period roughly equal to the second trimester, the state may, if it chooses, regulate the abortion procedure for reasons affecting the mother's health. 3. For the stage subsequent to viability—approximately the third trimester—the state may regulate and even forbid abortion, except in cases where medical opinion deems it necessary to preserve the life of the mother.

The second major decision is *Planned Parenthood of Central Missouri v. Danforth*,[2] issued on July 1, 1976. In this case, the Supreme Court reviewed two sections of the Missouri abortion statute. One stated that during the first trimester the husband's written consent was required unless the woman's life was endangered by the pregnancy. Here the Court held that the state may not constitutionally require his consent, for it cannot delegate to the spouse a veto power which it does not have. Since the state is not permitted to veto first trimester abortion, neither is anyone else. In virtue of this ruling, Evelyn had the freedom to obtain an abortion whether John approved or not. Another section of the Missouri law required the written consent of parents or guardian if the woman is unmarried or under eighteen, unless the abortion is necessary to save her life. The Court declared this section unconstitutional for three reasons. First, as above, the state cannot grant to a third party a power which it does not have. Second, minors are protected by the Constitution and have constitutional rights. Third, although the state has broad authority to regulate activities of children, it should not give parents the power to overrule a decision made by the girl and her doctor, for this would neither strengthen family bonds nor enhance

[2]96 S. Ct. 2831.

parental authority when there is fundamental conflict and a weakening of the parent-child relationship. Thus, the Court concluded, any independent interest of the parents with regard to the continuing or termination of the pregnancy carries less weight than the right to privacy of a competent minor mature enough to become pregnant.

While the above two decisions were welcomed by the proponents of abortion and looked upon as victories, the third was something of a setback. In *Beal v. Doe*,[3] June 20, 1977, the justices held that states participating in the Medicaid program are not required to fund non-therapeutic abortions. They argued that Title 19 of the Social Security Act gives participating states broad discretionary powers in determining the extent of the medical assistance they will provide to Medicaid recipients, and requires only that the standards they set should be reasonable and consistent with the objectives of Title 19. Since non-therapeutic abortions are not necessary medical services, the refusal to fund them under Medicaid is not inconsistent with the objectives of Title 19. Thus it is up to each state to decide what it shall do in this particular situation. If Evelyn wanted an abortion but lived in a state which refused Medicaid funding, her final decision might depend on financial considerations.

Proponents of abortion feel that *Beal v. Doe* is, in effect, undermining the strength of the first two decisions. Opponents of abortion are generally heartened by it but are by no means satisfied; some are attempting to put forward a constitutional amendment which would forbid abortion for any reason. Both sides are engaged in intense lobbying. Consequently, although lawsuits and court decisions have clarified many of the legal aspects of abortion, there is no broad consensus on the question. Some legal questions have been settled, but not the moral or ethical issues. It is to considerations such as these that we now turn.

[3]97 S. Ct. 2366.

## THE QUESTION OF PERSONHOOD

One of the critical elements in the abortion debate is the issue of personhood. Is the fetus a person? When? The way you answer these two questions will affect your attitude toward abortion. Are we talking about a human being with a life and rights of its own, or about a conglomerate of cells that may be disposed of at the will or the convenience of the persons directly involved? Daniel Callahan, in his classic study of abortion, has identified three basic schools of opinion with respect to defining the status of the fetus: the *genetic school,* the *developmental school,* and the *school of social consequences.* [4]

The genetic school defines as human any being that has a genetic code. Since the genotype is set at the moment of fertilization, this means that the developing individual is human from the moment of conception. Further development and growth are simply the spelling out of what is written in the genetic code for this particular individual.

The developmental school holds that while fertilization establishes the genetic basis for an individual human being, some degree of development is necessary for an individual to be considered an individual human being. The developmentalists thus go a step beyond the geneticists and recognize a need for interaction between the genotype and the environment. This view suggests that one's genetic potential is not fully actualized until it has interacted in its own unique way with its environment, and thus opens up a fuller understanding of the whole range of human attributes.

The school of social consequences shifts the question from "When does life begin?" to "When does *human* life begin?" According to this group, the fetus is to be defined on the basis of the social consequences of that decision. If defining a certain kind of fetus as human creates problems, then perhaps that class of fetuses should not be so defined. In setting social

[4]Daniel Callahan, *Abortion: Law, Choice and Morality, op. cit.,* pp. 378ff.

policy, they begin with the question "What kind of people do we want?" and then define individuals accordingly. From this perspective, what is important is not the biological or developmental dimension, but the desires of society in terms of social and moral policy.

Each of these groups brings a distinctive point of view to the task of defining a fetus and of making moral decisions in its regard. Depending on which school you gravitate to, your position on abortion will vary significantly. A consideration of these three orientations provides a context from which to begin thinking about abortion. The final decision reached by John and Evelyn will probably be influenced by the way they think of their newly conceived child—as already a human being, or as a potential person, or as a being whose identity and worth are totally subject to society's and their own preferences.

## SANCTITY OF LIFE

Another major element in the abortion debate is the concept of the sanctity of life. It includes several dimensions, each of which plays an important role in evaluating the ethics of abortion, for many conflicting values need to be weighed in attempting to reconcile a variety of competing interests.

Sanctity of life[5] includes the following elements:

• *Survival of the human species*. Humans ought to work for the survival, not the destruction of the race.

• *Survival of family lineage*. Families should be free to determine their own size.

• *Respect for physical (bodily) life*. People ought to have the assurance of being protected by fellow humans.

• *Respect for self-determination*. Persons should be free to exercise personal choice and to make decisions about matters that affect their own welfare.

---

[5]*Ibid.*, pp. 307ff.

• *Respect for bodily wholeness.* Individuals should be protected from having their bodies violated.

The last two elements, respect for personal choice and bodily wholeness, must be weighed on the scale with reverence for bodily life and the survival of the human species. It is obvious that abortions decrease the number of humans; it is not obvious that, even in large numbers, they threaten the survival of the species. On the other hand, the fetus is an existing individual possessing a human genotype; of what value is that when weighed against the woman's right to make decisions regarding her own destiny and her personal bodily integrity? The battle lines in the abortion controversy are not always drawn between those who acknowledge the sanctity of life and those who do not; sometimes it is their very reverence for life that makes them adversaries as they attempt to reconcile the many and often competing dimensions of the sanctity of life.

Another problem associated with the concept of the sanctity of life is the history of the way in which that concept has been applied to moral problems. Roman Catholicism, for example, has always taken this idea very seriously, and some present-day Roman Catholics, in opposing abortion, see themselves as waging the latest in a long line of battles against those who value life less than they do. There may be some truth in this view, but the historical reality is not quite so simple. As a matter of fact, Catholic moral theology has made some significant compromises over the years. For example, it has argued consistently that the state has the right to take the life of a criminal. To be sure, there have always been some Catholic thinkers who have opposed capital punishment, perhaps more today than ever; nevertheless, opposition to the death penalty is certainly not a characteristically Catholic attitude. Roman Catholicism also has a long history of supporting the traditional teaching of the just war, which implies that killing is legitimate under certain conditions, and it has argued for the validity of self-defense, which would include taking the life of the unjust aggressor if that were the only way to preserve one's own life. Again, there have been exceptions in these last two cases; a small but significant minority of Catholics have espoused pacifism and rejected all killing in the name of self-defense, including the so-called just war. But while pacifists have usually been respected and even honored within the Catholic community, their position has never been considered normative. In other words, a Catholic may be against all taking of life but does not have to take that stand in order to be considered a Catholic.

Thus Roman Catholic ethics has, for centuries, granted certain exceptions to its ban against violating the sacredness of human life. With respect to abortion, however, it has argued that one class of individuals—the fetus, broadly understood—has an absolute right to life—a right that may never be violated directly for any reason whatsoever. Such a position is variously supported by a basic appeal to the genetic school, the defenselessness of the fetus, the right to life of each individual, and the authority of the Church.[6] While not arbitrary, this interpretation of the sanctity of life is at least selective. Therefore, when we evaluate the principle of the sanctity of life as it affects abortion, we must remember that it has been applied more strictly here than in other life-and-death disputes.

## THREE BASIC POSITIONS

There are three basic positions on abortion: the conservative, the liberal, and the moderate.[7] The conservative position holds that under no circumstances may abortions be performed and offers a variety of religious and philosophic reasons. These include the concept of the absolute sanctity of life,

---

[6]Strictly speaking, of course, the Chruch does not argue from its authority as such, but from what it considers the intrinsic morality of abortion. Nevertheless, in the minds of at least some Catholics, the weight of the Church's authority reinforces its moral stand.

[7]James Nelson, *Human Medicine*, Minneapolis: Augsburg Publishing House, 1973, pp. 31ff.

the inviolability of an innocent human being, the traditional Catholic teaching that an embryo and a fetus are human beings from the first moment of conception and therefore may not be violated,[8] and, finally, the fear that a pro-abortion policy may open the door to the destruction of unwanted persons like the handicapped and the aged. The liberals, on the other hand, claim that abortion is justified for any one of several reasons. These include the quality of life for the fetus, the mother's health, her career, the right to control her own body, and the economic condition of the family. The question of whether the fetus has moral value or not is answered by the overriding rights and claims of the woman.

The moderates seek a middle ground between these two positions. They recognize the legitimacy of abortion in certain situations, but never without suffering and pain on the part of both the fetus and the parents. The fetus has rights, but so does the woman, and when these rights conflict, the decision will entail suffering and guilt. It is a tragic choice but it must be made in a way that will cause the least amount of evil possible. Thus the moderates permit abortion only under a narrowly defined set of circumstances, and always with a sense of tragedy and loss.

Whatever decision John and Evelyn make, it will probably reflect one or more of these three positions. The conservative view would clearly prohibit abortion in her case. To the liberals, there would be no solid reasons against abortion, and several in favor of it. The more nuanced moderate position would leave it up to them to weigh the factors involved and decide which course would be the lesser evil.

## TWO WORLD VIEWS

What is the source of these profound disagreements? Gregory Baum sees them proceeding from the radically differ-

[8]With the advance of biology and medical science, Catholic theologians have recognized that the moment that the embryo or fetus becomes a person is problematic. They are in general agreement that, with conception, a process begins which will issue in a human person. Hence, the embryo or fetus is at least potentially a person.

ent outlooks on nature and sexuality.[9] The first sees sexuality and reproduction as a part of nature watched over by divine providence. In this perspective, sexuality is seen primarily as a biological function which, while having pleasure attached to it, has as one of its primary purposes the begetting of children. And since nature is watched over by God's providence, to practice birth control or to obtain an abortion is interfering with this order of nature and is therefore sinful. In the second world view, God's providence is seen not as expressed through nature but as a gracious action within human life which enables people to take greater responsibility for themselves and their environment. Sexuality is more than biology; it is a human reality with many meanings and purposes. Birth control for family planning is looked upon not as sinful but as an exercise of responsible parenthood. And abortion may be practiced as a means of taking responsibility for one's own destiny and for the future.

Not everyone would accept Baum's description of these two world views as complete. Many feel that the second view, which stresses human responsibility, does not necessarily lead to a permissive attitude toward abortion. They claim that the exercise of responsibility, in this case, consists precisely in recognizing and respecting the fetus' right to life. But Baum is certainly correct in pointing out that an attitude of self-responsibility is more likely to dispose one to consider seriously such initiatives as contraception and abortion.

Such diverse outlooks on the meaning and purpose of life are often unstated, but they seriously affect the way we understand ourselves and interpret the limits of our responsibility. Such deeply embedded outlooks and attitudes are not easily changed and cannot easily be compromised. When people face the kind of choices that confronted John and Evelyn, their final decision will probably be determined in whole or in part by whichever of these two world views is predominant in their thinking and feeling. For they represent the ultimate founda-

---

[9]Gregory Baum, "Abortion: An Ecumenical Dilemma," in T. A. Shannon, editor, *Bioethics*, New York: Paulist Press, 1976, pp. 25ff.

tion upon which the abortion issue will continue to be debated for years to come.

## TOPICS FOR DISCUSSION

1. Anti-abortionists accuse their opponents of a lack of reverence for the sanctity of life. To what extent is this charge justified?

2. How do Church teachings on war and capital punishment affect Catholics' anti-abortion arguments based on reverence for life?

3. Catholics insist that their opposition to abortion is not based on a religious doctrine and hence should not be viewed as an attempt to impose their religious convictions on others. Explain and evaluate this position.

4. List what you consider one *strength* and one *weakness* in each of the three schools of opinion regarding the status of the fetus—the genetic, the developmental, and the school of social consequences.

5. The *moderate* position on abortion tries to incorporate the strengths and to eliminate the weaknesses of both the conservative and the liberal positions. Do you feel that it succeeds? Explain.

6. What advice would you give John and Evelyn? What reasons would you give?

## RESOURCES

Callahan, Daniel. *Abortion: Law, Choice and Morality.* New York: Macmillan, 1970.

Griesez, Germaine G. *Abortion: The Myths, the Realities and the Arguments.* New York: World Publishing Company, 1970.

Mohr, James C. *Abortion in America: The Origins and the Evolution of National Policy.* New York: Oxford University Press, 1978.

Noonan, John T., Jr. *The Morality of Abortion: Legal and Historical Perspectives.* Cambridge: Harvard University Press, 1970.

Perkins, Robert L., editor. *Abortion: Pro and Con.* Cambridge: Schenckman Publishing Company, 1974.

Potts, Malcolm, Peter Diggory, and John Peel. *Abortion.* Cambridge: Cambridge University Press, 1977.

Walbert, David F., and J. Douglas Butler, editors. *Abortion, Society and the Law.* Cleveland: The Press of Case Western Reserve University, 1973.

*Abortion and the Law.* Black and white. 16mm. 54 minutes. No charge. Distributor: Cuyahoga County Public Library, 4510 Memphis Ave., Cleveland, Ohio.

*Conversations in Medical Ethics: Abortion.* Black and white. 16mm. 10 minutes. Rent: Free to physicians. Distributor: Student American Medical Association, 2635 Flossmoor Rd., Flossmoor, Illinois 60422.

*Intra-Uterine Diagnosis in Early Pregnancy: Fetal, Parental and Societal Considerations.* Black and white. 3/4" Video cassette. 60 minutes. Sale: $68. Distributor: Dr. Bernard Towers, Department of Pediatrics, School of Medicine, U.C.L.A., Los Angeles, Calif. 90024.

*Chapter Five*

---

# DEFINITION OF DEATH

Death is humanity's oldest and most feared enemy. In struggling against it we always lose the war, but lately we have been winning some of the battles in impressive fashion. Between 1900 and 1975, the average life span of Americans rose from forty-three to seventy-one years. Eliminating many diseases has helped to increase our life expectancy, but our major success has been our ability to prolong the process of dying. The intensive care unit is a symbol at once of medical technology's highest achievements and its most poignant failure. Our power to postpone the inevitable has shown us that, in many ways, we are no closer to understanding or dealing with death than were our medically unsophisticated ancestors.

The technological culture in which we live has raised a host of problems with respect to death, not the least of which is that of defining death itself. If we succeed through technology in prolonging the dying process, we are by that same process prolonging life. But when can we say that life is over and that death has ensued? Defining death used to be easy; when the heart stopped beating and breathing ceased, life was over. But now when a respirator can do a patient's breathing, how alive can that person be said to be? How can we know when to start such a process and when to stop it? What kind of death are we talking about?

There are several different definitions of death from various points of view. In physical terms, a person is dead when the heart has stopped beating. From a spiritual point of view, death means the separation of soul and body, the absolute departure of a transcendent principle from an individual's life. In psychological terms, people are dead when they have completely turned in on themselves and want no human contact. From the point of view of brain activity, death can be declared when no activity is recordable on the electroencephalogram. Finally, there is the cellular definition of death, which consists in the disintegration and breakdown of the basic metabolic processes of the body's substance.

## FOUR APPROACHES TO DEFINITION

Robert M. Veatch[1] has recently provided an excellent framework for classifying definitions of death according to three elements: the concept of death, the locus of death, and the criteria employed.

Definition one on Veatch's list is the traditional understanding of death. Blood and breath are essential to the continuation of life; hence, when people stop breathing and there is no pulse, they are pronounced dead. Such a definition is complicated by the use of a mechanical respirator which can keep blood and oxygen circulating almost indefinitely.

Definition two is a religious or philosophical definition associated with Roman Catholic thought. It is derived from a

---

[1]Robert Veatch, *Death, Dying, and the Biological Revolution*, New Haven: Yale University Press, 1976, pp. 21ff.

# LEVELS OF THE DEFINITION OF DEATH *

**FORMAL DEFINITION: Death means a complete change in the status of a living entity characterized by the irreversible loss of those characteristics that are essentially significant to it.**

| Concept of death: | Locus of death: | Criteria of death: |
|---|---|---|
| philosophical or theological judgment of the essentially significant change at death. | place to look to determine if a person has died. | measurements physicians or other officials use to determine whether a person is dead—to be determined by scientific empirical study. |
| 1. The irreversible stopping of the flow of "vital" body fluids, i.e., the blood and breath | Heart and lungs | 1. Visual observation of respiration, perhaps with the use of a mirror<br>2. Feeling of the pulse, possibly supported by electrocardiogram |
| 2. The irreversible loss of the soul from the body | The pineal body? (according to Descartes) The respiratory track? | Observation of breath? |
| 3. The irreversible loss of the capacity for bodily integration and social interaction | The brain | 1. Unreceptivity and unresponsivity<br>2. No movements or breathing<br>3. No reflexes (except spinal reflexes)<br>4. Flat electroencephalogram (to be used as confirmatory evidence)<br>—All tests to be repeated 24 hours later (excluded conditions: hypothermia and central nervous system drug depression) |
| 4. Irreversible loss of consciousness or the capacity for social interaction | Probably the neocortex | Electroencephalogram |

*Note:* The possible concepts, loci, and criteria of death are much more complex than the ones given here. These are meant to be simplified models of types of positions being taken in the current debate. It is obvious that those who believe that death means the irreversible loss of the capacity for bodily integration (3) or the irreversible loss of consciousness (4) will have no reservations about pronouncing death when the heart and lungs have ceased to function. This is because they are willing to use loss of heart and lung activity as a shortcut criteria for death, believing that once heart and lungs have stopped, the brain or neocortex will necessarily stop as well.

* Robert M. Veatch. *Death, Dying and the Biological Revolution*

traditional way of defining the human person as a substantial unity with two dimensions, body and soul (or matter and form). The soul is viewed as higher than the body and needed to animate the body, i.e., to give it the distinctively human qualities of rationality and freedom. Thus, when the soul leaves the body the person no longer exists; death has occurred because the substantial union of body and soul has been dissolved. The problem with this definition is knowing whether or not the soul has left the body. One could fall back on the philosophical maxim, "Action follows being," and argue that when an individual no longer acted as a human, then the substantial unity had been dissolved and death had occurred. Roman Catholic pastoral practice, however, followed much safer lines. Priests were permitted to administer the sacraments of anointing and reconciliation several hours after the official pronouncement of death, especially when death was sudden or violent. In such cases the sacraments were to be administered conditionally, of course, but the practice was based on the realization that one could not know the precise time of the soul's departure from the body. The general medical criteria for definition one were accepted for pronouncing death, but some leeway was built into the practice of administering the last rites because of uncertainty about the precise time of the soul's departure.

Definitions three and four have arisen primarily from the application of technology to medical practice. We now have the ability to maintain artificially the action of heart and lungs. Thus, if a patient is on a respirator and oxygen and blood are circulating, the criteria of definition one cannot be applied. Another reason for shifting to these definitions is the frequent occurrence of irreversible coma. In this condition, thanks to life support machines, the patient is breathing and the heart is pumping blood, but consciousness has been irrevocably lost, and with it the capacity for bodily or social integration. The individual has lost elements perceived as critical to the contemporary understanding of human existence. These are some of the reasons for trying to find more suitable criteria for defining death.

Definition three employs the most famous and widely used of these norms, drawn up by a committee of the Harvard Medical School in 1969.[2] These criteria—unreceptivity and unresponsiveness, no movement or breathing, no reflexes, and the confirmation of these by an electroencephalogram—seek to develop measurements which will predict a total and irreversible lack of activity in the brain. Underlying these criteria is a particular concept of death: the irreversible loss of the capacity for bodily and social integration. The death of the total brain (brain-stem, spinal cord, and neo-cortex) eliminates the bodily dimension that is a necessary precondition for social integration. In this perspective, the flat EEG only confirms what is known from the first three criteria.

However, when the focus of attention shifts to consciousness and social interaction, then the Harvard criteria become too conservative. Even when there is a flat EEG, some basic responses such as breathing and heartbeat may continue. Thus definition four looks to the irreversible loss of neo-cortical activity as the only significant criterion, because it eliminates all capacity for consciousness and renders impossible all social integration. Thus the only test needed to be performed is the EEG. This creates the paradoxical situation, noted by Veatch, that someone could be alive according to the Harvard norms but dead according to the neo-cortical criterion. Thus the Harvard criteria may suffer from the same difficulties as the traditional heart and lung definition: the problem of declaring dead someone who is breathing and whose heart is beating. Of course, what is critical is the place one selects to look for death: the biological (definitions one and two), the biological and social (definition three), or the social (definition four).

[2] Ad Hoc Committee of the Harvard Medical School, "A Definition of Irreversible Coma," *Journal* of the American Medical Association 205:337-40, August 1968.

All these considerations put a great strain on human reason and on the resources of health-care professions, families, and patients. Nevertheless, discussions of these definitions of death and their applicability to patients are occurring more and more frequently. It is becoming increasingly difficult to die a so-called natural death at home or elsewhere. Most people now die in a variety of institutional settings which have many death-prolonging or life-span-extending technologies at their disposal. These instruments have the capacity to prolong life, but are not necessarily able to cure the illness or disease. Thus there comes a time when we must ask whether the patient under treatment is dead or alive.

## THE LIMITS OF RESPONSIBILITY

At this point we confront the limits of human responsibility. We may not want to make such life-and-death decisions, and we may feel that it is not proper for humans to exercise such power, but it is becoming increasingly clear that we have no other choice. There are limits to what medicine can do, and hence limits to curing. However, as Paul Ramsey observes, there are no limits to caring.[3] To assume the awesome responsibility of defining death may well be a gesture of care for those who are being maintained only by artificial means.

A common objection to such action is that in redefining death we are playing God. This is based on the traditional view that God is the author of life and death. Hence one's death is God's responsibility, and any interference with this is overstepping the bounds of human responsibility. However, such a view also assumes, often enough uncritically, that God is directly involved with the very maintenance of all the physical and biological processes of the universe. While wishing to avoid the deist view of God as a Creator who sets the universe in motion and then has nothing further to do with it,

[3]Paul Ramsey, *The Patient as Person, op. cit.*, pp. 113ff.

we must also avoid the contrary error of assuming that God has everything to do with the running of the world. The former view overstates human responsibility; the latter view devalues it.

A second problem associated with defining death concerns the expression of value preferences. A bewildering profusion of physical, social, religious, and personal considerations compete for attention. To which, if any, should we give priority? What are the relationships among these various elements? Will the consequences of defining death lead us in directions we may not wish to go? Yet we cannot afford to be paralyzed by indecision, for there are great risks involved in *not* deciding. We are faced with patients who are unresponsive to a variety of stimuli and who demonstrate no consciousness, but who may be still breathing, with or without assistance. Presently many of these persons are confined to a kind of medical limbo—not quite dead, but not quite alive either. We care about them, but we cannot cure them. We can maintain them and prolong the death that comes to all, but is this acting responsibly? Is this treatment for the sake of treatment? And when people persist, saying they hope for a miracle, are they simply avoiding facing up to the situation? Are they really expressing a naive, uncritical faith in the possibilities of science, technology, and medicine?

A third problem has to do with the religious interpretation of suffering. Although it is recognized as an evil and as one of the major problems of human existence, theological tradition has sought to find meaning in suffering by relating it to other human and divine experiences. Suffering can mold character. It places sober but needed limitations on human expectations. Christian tradition, especially, sees it as potentially a spiritually transforming experience: a way of atoning for sin, a stimulus to spiritual growth, or a means of continuing redemption by identifying with the suffering Christ. In this sense, suffering can indeed be a redemptive experience, an occasion for deep personal growth and the strengthening of the community. Yet there also seems to be such a thing as unredemptive suffering. When the sufferer is unconscious or in a coma, it is impossible to personalize the situation and to place the experience within a meaningful human or religious perspective. Thus even though one may be inclined to make illness a spiritual experience, the capacity for doing so is absent and often irretrievably lost. Family members can hardly make religious sense of the situation because they cannot interact with the patient. They can personalize the situation to some degree but not totally, for a key element in such an interpretation—the patient—is absent. When the people involved can make little or no sense of the situation, it will not contribute to growth. Instead, it may grow cancer-like, spread and become all-encompassing and lead to the destruction of all concerned.

## A LEGITIMATE ENTERPRISE

When we reflect on the doctrine of human stewardship over the world, the limits of medicine, and the inability to retrieve anything positive from some situations, we recognize the need to re-evaluate the definition of death that is operative in the practice of contemporary medicine. Understandably, many fear the risks involved in using criteria other than the traditional heart and lung definition. But the problems created by the increasing technological capacity of modern medicine demand a response, and this one is both appropriate and responsible. Such efforts are not attempts to devalue or deny the right to life of the terminally ill or of those in irreversible coma. They are not attempts to set in motion a process to remove systematically such individuals from society. Nor are they attempts of one group to gain ultimate control over others.

The attempt to redefine death in the contemporary practice of medicine has much to recommend it. First, it recognizes the limits of medical ability to cure. In spite of the best care and the most devoted healing efforts, there are some patients who are unresponsive and unable to benefit therefrom. Second, it tries to resolve the many painful, tragic, and meaningless experiences that occur when a person is in this medical-moral limbo. By recognizing limits and admitting that sometimes all we can do is prolong the dying process, it seeks in a redefinition of death a means to terminate a therapy that cannot cure. Third, it is a proper exercise of human responsibility. We need to make more precise something that we all recognize as a fact of human experience—death—and to do it within the context of contemporary medicine with its technological dimension. In doing so, we are not assuming God-like power. If we thought that God was directly responsible for all physical and biological processes, we would never do anything to interfere in any way with these processes—which is absurd. Moreover, redefining death does not interfere in these processes; rather, it is an attempt to recognize the end of them. True, redefining death may possibly imply the removal or cessation of therapy; but it does not necessarily imply intervention to bring a process to an end.

Contemporary medical practice, which enables us to prolong artificially the circulation of oxygen and blood, has brought us to a situation in which we often find it difficult to recognize death. To respond to this situation, many are convinced that we must try to find a new definition of death. Such an attempt acknowledges the limits of medicine and the fact that even when we cannot cure we are always bound to care. It confronts the experience of irreversible coma as a medical-moral limbo that is meaningless and unredemptive to both patient and family. For all of these reasons, such redefinition is responsible and morally sound.

## TOPICS FOR DISCUSSION

1. Why has it become difficult to define death, when it used to be so easy?

2. Some of those who resist the notion of redefining death

object that in so doing we would be "playing God." What do they mean? How do the authors answer this objection?

3. Rank Veatch's four definitions of death, 1, 2, 3, and 4 in the order of your preference. Explain the reasons for your selections.

4. What are some of the social dangers involved in redefining death?

5. What are the dangers involved in refusing to redefine death?

6. A 56-year-old laborer fell and suffered a massive brain injury. Surgeons performed an emergency craniotomy and placed him on a respirator which kept him "mechanically alive." His body temperature, pulse, blood pressure, and respiration were, for the most part, normal. But an EEG shows flat lines, offering no clinical evidence of viability or cortical activity. The respirator was cut off and the patient pronounced dead. His heart and kidneys were then removed and transplanted in another patient. The dead man's brother sued for damages, charging a deliberate plot to use his heart and the hastening of his death by shutting off the mechanical means of support.[4]

If you were on the jury, how would you vote?

## RESOURCES

Committee on Evolving Trends in Society Affecting Life. *Death and Dying: Determining and Defining Death—A Compilation of Definitions, Selected Readings and Bibliography.* San Francisco: California Medical Association, 1975.

Harvard Medical School, Ad Hoc Committee of the Harvard Medical School to Examine the Definition of Brain Death. "A Definition of Irreversible Coma." *Journal* of the American Medical Association 205 (1968), 337–40.

Institute of Society, Ethics and the Life Sciences, Task Force

[4]Robert Veatch, *Case Studies in Bioethics*, Cambridge: Harvard University Press, pp. 319ff.

on Death and Dying. "Refinements in Criteria for the Determination of Death." *Journal* of the American Medical Association 221 (July 9, 1972), 48–53.

Isaacs, Leonard. "Death, Where Is Thy Distinguishing?" Hastings Center *Report* 8 (February 6, 1978), 5–8.

Veith, Frank J., *et al.* "Brain Death: Part 1: A Status Report of Medical and Ethical Considerations." "Part 2: A Status Report of Legal Considerations." *Journal* of the American Medical Association 238 (October 10 and 17, 1977), 1651–55 and 1744–48.

*Death*. Black and white. 16 mm. Rent $35. Sale $275. Distributor: Filmmakers Library, Inc., 290 West End Ave., New York, New York 10020.

*To Die Today*. Black and white. 16 mm. 50 minutes. Rent $35. Sale $275. Distributor: Filmmakers Library, Inc., 290 West End Ave., New York, New York 10020.

*Must We Redefine Death?* Black and white. 3/4" Videocassette. 60 minutes. Sale $68. Distributor: Dr. Bernard Towers, Department of Pediatrics, School of Medicine, U.C.L.A., Los Angeles, Calif. 90024.

*Chapter Six*

---

# EUTHANASIA

A physicist who had done research on X-rays for thirty years was suffering terribly from skin cancer. Part of his jaw, his upper lip, nose and left hand were lost; growths had been removed from his right arm and two fingers from his right hand. He was blind and in constant, excruciating pain. Only surgery and continued suffering awaited the patient, who the doctors felt had about a year to live. For months he pleaded with his three younger brothers to put an end to his life. Eventually, the youngest, a man of thirty-six took a pistol and, after an afternoon and early evening of wandering and drinking in local bars, returned to the hospital during visiting hours and shot his brother to death.

In proposing a bill in the British Parliament in 1936, Lord Moynihan suggested that when there was advanced or fatal disease and when the pain could no longer be endured or controlled, active or direct euthanasia could be administered.[1] If his motion had been carried and enacted into law, patients like the physicist could have legally asked for what the Oxford English Dictionary, in defining euthanasia, calls "the action of inducing a quiet and easy death." Webster's 1976 New International Dictionary defines it as "an act or practice of painlessly putting to death persons suffering from incurable conditions or disease."

The issue is raised not only by patients suffering from painful and debilitating, terminal diseases. Now that we can prolong the dying process by applying technology to medicine, we see many people surviving, but with physical signs of life that are minimal and artificially maintained. Why not, many ask, intervene in the name of mercy to end a life which can only hope for death as a release?

The definitions we use may affect our response. Moynihan's definition uses the language of rights, suggesting that individuals may be *entitled* to euthanasia, i.e., they may have a moral claim either on ending their life or having it ended for them. The focus here is on pain, suffering, and an incurable disease as critical elements in a pro-euthanasia decision. Similarly, Webster's definition focuses on euthanasia as a way out of intractable suffering resulting from an incurable condition. The Oxford definition is the most radical of all, for it simply talks of a quiet and easy death without discussing the context in which that death would occur. In this approach, any reason might be used to justify euthanasia, and not just the traditional motive of relieving suffering.

These definitions, regardless of any strengths or weaknesses they may have, raise two critical questions: 1. In the event of a terminal illness, may the patient or someone else actively intervene to end the patient's life? 2. Is the withdrawal of treatment a form of euthanasia?

In some respects, the problem of active or direct euthana-

---

[1]Robert Veatch, *Death, Dying and the Biological Revolution, op. cit.*, p. 186.

sia raises questions similar to those posed by suicide, but there are some differences. People who take their own lives usually do so for non-medical reasons. As a rule, suicide is an interruption of the life process rather than an acceleration of imminent or certain death. Also, the one committing suicide is the sole and exclusive cause of his or her own death. Because the context is usually non-medical and because people usually take their own lives by themselves, the ethics of direct euthanasia should be treated separately from the ethics of suicide.

## DIRECT EUTHANASIA

Many fear that the acceptance of euthanasia will open the floodgates to a host of social abuses and immoral practices. Some see this issue as an outgrowth of the abortion debate. If we are allowed to rid ourselves, before birth, of those who are undesirable, why may we not do the same with old or sick people who are unproductive and undesirable? Some argue that direct euthanasia is always wrong, whether requested by the patient or not. They reason that since God is the Creator, he alone has full dominion over life and death, and that while humans have proper responsibility in this world, their stewardship does not extend to ending life, no matter what their reasons. Indeed, there has always been a moral consensus against intervening to end people's lives, and this has been strengthened by the bitter memory of the holocaust, which must never be allowed to happen again. Others fear that the potential for abuse is too great: if today we relieve helpless sufferers, tomorrow someone will use the precedent to get rid of burdensome, "useless" people. Then, too, there is the witness of many religions which base their arguments against direct euthanasia on the traditions of the sanctity of life and the prohibition against taking innocent life. Others simply argue that direct euthanasia, performed by someone acting for the patient, is homicide and therefore both ethically and legally prohibited. They are right, of course, even though there have been no *successful* prosecutions of mercy killers. Finally, it is argued that if direct euthanasia by an agent is allowed, it is the physician who is most often going to play this role. This goes contrary to the traditions of the medical profession, which have always called upon the doctor to cure, not to kill. And what would happen to the critical element of trust in the physician-patient relationship? Seriously ill persons may avoid seeking treatment if they know that doctors can aid in direct euthanasia.

On the other side, there are several arguments offered in favor of direct euthanasia. If a patient suffers from a terminal illness, why not choose death now rather than later, since it is inevitable anyway? When the patient is in great pain or in an irreversible coma, and nothing can be done except administering pain-killing drugs, why not put an end to the suffering and the misery? The patient's family, too, must be considered. Terminal illnesses and their treatment may cause genuine personal difficulties and unreasonable economic hardship. The relatives' helplessness and inability to do anything meaningful for a loved one can cause pain and suffering as great as that endured by the dying person. And the skyrocketing cost of medical treatment can destroy a family and its resources. Care of other family members may be neglected, raising the question of fairness and justice. Finally, it is seriously argued by some that physical life in itself is not the highest good. Rather, it is important insofar as it is a pre-condition for actualizing and realizing other values such as love, friendship, and socialization. From this perspective, direct euthanasia would be justified because the patient's condition makes it impossible to achieve what is humanly valuable.

## INDIRECT EUTHANASIA

Another set of problems is raised by the withholding of treatment or by stopping treament already begun. This practice, known as indirect or passive euthanasia, has been accepted by most people and by most religious teachings. Justification is based on the traditional principle that we are morally bound to use only the ordinary means of medical care and may refuse those which are extraordinary. The latter are defined as all medicines, treatments, and operations which cannot be obtained or used without excessive expense, pain, or other inconvenience for the patients or for others, or which if used would not offer reasonable hope of benefit to the person.[2]

A case in point was that of an eleven-year-old boy who was dying of cystic fibrosis. Barring a miracle, the medical staff knew that only a few months were left. Two weeks previously, he had been brought to the hospital in an acute respiratory crisis, the fifth such attack in the last six months. He had been in and out of the hospital for the last two years. His condition was aggravated by bronchial infection, lung abscesses, and massive salt depletion, so penicillin therapy and intravenous saline were ordered. Emphysema and bronchopneumonia contributed to a rapidly deteriorating condition. The staff agreed that bronchoscopy, a difficult and only occasionally helpful procedure, offered the only chance of keeping the boy alive. At this point the mother intervened, insisting that the treatment be stopped. "Just maintain him," she said, "and let him die in peace."

During an emergency meeting of the medical staff, one doctor urged them to grant the mother's wish and let the boy die peacefully. Others replied: "The fundamental task of medicine is to preserve the life and health of the patient. We just cannot refuse to provide the well-established procedures which will possibly save his life, even if only for a few days or weeks."

The tradition which permits indirect euthanasia affirms that there are things we should do to maintain our health, but that there are limits to these. One need not do everything

---

[2]Gerald Kelly, S.J., *Medical-Moral Problems, op. cit.*, pp. 129ff.

possible to gain a minimal result or to increase one's life-span by a few weeks. A proposed treatment may not offer hope of any reasonable benefit. It may simply be too expensive—e.g., heart surgery—or it may cause serious inconvenience, as chemotherapy sometimes does. In such cases, one is not obliged to use that treatment, or the patient may request that it be withdrawn.

Up to this point we have spoken of direct and indirect euthanasia as if they were clearly distinct. Some proponents of direct euthanasia, however, do not admit the difference. They claim that withdrawing treatment is the same as directly intervening to end a person's life. Hence there is no basic moral difference between the two acts, and if withdrawal of treatment is permitted, so should direct euthanasia.[3] The literature indicates that the experts have not fully resolved this dispute, but some points are clear. First, the cause of death is different. In the case of withdrawal of treatment, the cause is the illness and its many surrounding effects. In active euthanasia, the direct cause of death is not the illness but the action taken with the purpose of ending the patient's life. Second, the intention is different. In direct euthanasia, the intention is to end the person's life. In withdrawal of treatment, the intention is to let the illness or disease run its course to its natural conclusion. Two points need to be made here. First, the intention behind withdrawing treatment may be to get rid of a troublesome situation—i.e., the patient—and thus the intention may be very reprehensible. On the other hand, it may be the recognition that we have done all we can and that all further efforts would be futile and should be stopped. Second, there are some things in life that are beyond our control, and death seems to be one of these. But knowing that people must die does not necessarily imply that we may directly intervene to end life. Thus, while there may be some

[3]James Rachels, "Active and Passive Euthanasia," *New England Journal of Medicine*, 292:78 (January 1975).

things we cannot control—the full range and the effects of a disease—there may also be things we perhaps ought not to control—the agency and circumstances of another's death.

## CRITICAL ISSUES

Thus death and dying present us with some of the most critical problems of our time: our ability to prolong life, our ability to prolong dying, the knowledge of the limits of modern medicine, the uncertainty about the limits of our responsibility, and the certainty of our obligation to care. All of these elements, combined with the enormous personal and emotional conflicts that occur during the dying process, lead to some of the most trying and soul-searching dilemmas we can know. As technology continues to be applied to medicine and individuals can be maintained for longer and longer periods with no hope of recovery in sight, the dilemmas will increase in intensity. The debate over the limits of human responsibility will escalate. A perception of limits and a consensus on them will be hard to come by. And the problem will be magnified.

The traditional approach recognizes that not everything need be done when hope is rapidly disappearing. Although formulated at a time when medicine was much less sophisticated than today and much more conscious of its limits, perhaps it may be time to apply its wisdom to our situation in which medicine is indeed much more highly developed but ultimately faces the same problems as did its ancient ancestors.

## TOPICS FOR DISCUSSION

1. What is the difference between euthanasia and suicide?

2. What is the difference between direct and indirect euthanasia?

3. What are the social risks involved in permitting direct euthanasia?

4. What are the arguments in favor of active euthanasia? Do you find them persuasive?

5. How does the traditional distinction between ordinary and extraordinary treatment affect this controversy?

6. In the case of the mother of the dying boy, do you think the doctors should have acceded to her request to cease treatment? Why:

7. If you had been on the jury trying the physicist's brother, would you have voted for acquittal or for conviction? Why?

## RESOURCES

Behnke, John A., and Sissela Bok. *The Dilemmas of Euthanasia*. New York: Doubleday Anchor, 1975.

Cahill, Lisa S. "A 'Natural Law' Reconsideration of Euthanasia." *Linacre Quarterly* 44 (February 1977), 47–63.

Cantor, Norman L. "The Patient's Decision To Decline Life Saving Medical Treatment: Bodily Integrity versus the Preservation of Life." *Rutgers Law Review* 26 (Winter 1972), 228–64.

Downing, A. B. *Euthanasia and the Right To Die*. New York: Humanities Press, 1970.

Horan, Dennis J., and David Mall, editors. *Death, Dying and Euthanasia*. Washington, D.C.: University Publications of America, 1977.

Maguire, Daniel C. *Death by Choice*. New York: Doubleday, 1974.

Mannes, Marya. *Last Rights*. New York: William Morrow and Company, 1974.

Rachels, James. "Active and Passive Euthanasia." *New England Journal of Medicine* 292 (January 9, 1975), 78–80.

Russell, O. Ruth. *Freedom To Die: Moral and Legal Aspects of Euthanasia*. New York: Human Sciences Press, 1975.

Sullivan, Thomas D. "Active and Passive Euthanasia: An Impertinent Distinction?" *Human Life Review* 3 (Summer 1977), 40–47.

Veatch, Robert M. *Death, Dying and the Biological Revolution.* New Haven: Yale University Press, 1976.

*How Could I Not Be Among You?* Color. 16 mm. 28 minutes. Rent: $37.50. Sale: $350. Distributor: The Eccentric Circle, P.O. Box 1481, Evanston, Illinois 60204.

*Please Let Me Die.* Color. Videocassette, videotape. 30 minutes. Rent: $25. Sale: $100. Distributor: Library of Clinical Psychiatric Syndromes, Dr. Robert B. White, Department of Psychiatry, University of Texas Medical Branch, Galveston, Texas 77550.

*Chapter Seven*

---

# THE LIVING WILL

Everyone agrees that we should make a will while we are of sound mind, so that our estate may be distributed fairly to those we leave behind. Now some are saying that it's time to include ourselves in that last will and testament. While we are competent, we could indicate our wishes about how we wish to be treated—or not treated—in the event of a teminal illness when we may be unconscious or otherwise unable to make a competent choice.

This device, known as the living will, is proposed as the solution to some of the difficult and complex problems described in the previous chapters. The Karen Ann Quinlan case has alerted us to the difficulty of making decisions about treating or withdrawing treatment from incompetent patients. When treatment seems only to maintain the patient rather than cause improvement or cure, what should we do? Who is to make the decision? How can we determine what is in the patient's best interest? These are the agonizing problems that almost always arise when age, physical condition., or lack of maturity renders patients unable to decide for themselves. And decisions must be made. Scarce resources, the cost of intensive care units, and the values and interests of the health care unit and the next of kin make it imperative that someone, somewhere make a life-or-death decision for someone else. The living will is an attempt to restore that responsibility to the person most directly affected—the patient.

The living will is based theoretically on the legal right that all competent persons have to refuse any treatment, and the teaching of several religious traditions that they have the moral right to refuse extraordinary treatment. Thus, the typical form of the will expresses a wish not to have heroic or extraordinary forms of treatment during a terminal illness or when death appears imminent. It also asks that medication be used to relieve pain even though it might shorten one's life. This is in keeping with an ethical principle accepted within Roman Catholicism and by many theologians and ethicians.[1] Thus, in terms of what is proposed, the living will is in harmony with both traditional and contemporary ethical teachings.

## RELATED PROBLEMS

What is novel, and therefore controversial, is the declaration of preference *before* the actual situation and the need for decision arises. This creates some practical problems. How do we know that the person who made the will hasn't changed his or her mind? Were the present circumstances envisioned when the will was made? What is the will's legal status? How does it bind the next of kin and the health care team and facility?

Of course, it is impossible to know whether patients have changed their minds if they are unconscious or incompetent. Evidence from recent conversations with relatives or friends

[1]Gerald Kelley, S.J., *Medical-Moral Problems, op. cit.,* pp. 129ff.

can help, but a direct answer is unobtainable. On the other hand, when people have taken the time and trouble to draw up or at least to sign such a will, we have some evidence of their seriousness of intent. In the absence of any contradictory evidence, it seems reasonable to respect such a statement. With regard to the problem of foreseeing the actual circumstances of the illness, what seems to matter is that the person refused therapies which would give no reasonable hope of recovery. The typical language of the living will generally looks to this one criterion: it is important to examine the possibility of recovery, not the kind of illness or its particular circumstances. Finally, no one challenges the idea of making a disposition, long before death, of money or property. Such dispositions, in fact, are considered socially responsible. People may argue over who ought to get how much or who should or should not be included in a will, but no one denies that the last will and testament remains binding after death in the absence of proper legal challenge. By the same token, it seems reasonable to accept a person's stated preferences concerning treatment in anticipation of future inability to make such decisions. This would allow the proper decision-maker to make the decision. It would relieve the family and the health care team of many agonizing pressures and problems. And it would eliminate the need for developing  many legal and bureaucratic structures to resolve such problems in the absence of a mechanism such as a living will.

The legal difficulties are harder to resolve. The original versions of the living will, distributed by the Euthanasia Educational Council, clearly indicated that such a document was not legally binding. More recent versions omit this particular phrase. Since there have been no court tests of the will's binding nature, its legal status is somewhat unclear.

## ATTEMPTS AT LEGISLATION

To remove this obscurity, various bills concerning right-to-die, death-with-dignity, and living wills have been introduced in state legislatures.[2] At this writing, about eighty-five pieces of legislation have been submitted. In 1977 alone, forty states were asked to consider such proposals. By that year, eight states—California, Idaho, Arkansas, New Mexico, Nevada, Oregon, Texas and North Carolina—had passed and enacted natural death acts. According to an analysis of these bills by Robert Veatch, they fall into three categories: (1) legalizing active euthanasia; (2) clarifying competent patients' rights; and (3) establishing decision-making processes for incompetent patients.

The first group of bills would apparently legalize active killing of the patient. Although they do not do so explicitly, they seem to imply that this would be an option. They require that the request be made voluntarily by an adult or a person over twenty-one years of age, suffering from an extremely painful terminal disease. In such a case euthanasia may be administered under the supervision either of a court or of a hospital panel, and the agent shall not be subject to prosecution for homicide. The apparent implicit allowance for active killing may possibly be due to a misunderstanding of the traditional distinction between active and passive euthanasia.

Bills of the second category, clarifying the rights of competent patients, follow the typical model of the living will as developed by the Euthanasia Education Council. Under their terms, competent patients would have the right to refuse certain kinds of medical treatment. These also attempt to answer such questions as: Do preferences stated while competent remain valid after the patient becomes incompetent? Who has the authority to interpret such instructions at that point? What penalties shall be imposed for failing to follow instructions? Does the refusal of life-saving treatment constitute evidence of incompetency?

The third group, while acknowledging the right of competent patients to make such decisions, consider the cases of

---

[2] Robert Veatch, "Analysis of Legislative Proposal on Euthanasia and Treatment Refusal," The Hastings Center: Hastings on Hudson, New York, 1977.

patients who have never been competent or who had not, while competent, expressed their wishes for treatment preferences. They indicate either that the authority of the physicians should be relied upon or that the next of kin or a similar agent should be empowered to make the decision. Veatch has proposed an alternative model bill stating that if a person is incompetent, decision-making authority should go to the one whom the patient, while competent, designated to be his or her agent. If no such person has been designated, then authority passes to the next of kin; if there are no relatives, it goes to a guardian appointed for that purpose by the court.[3]

## SHOULD SUCH BILLS BE PASSED?

Arguments for the necessity of such bills center around the tendency of physicians to treat even when treatment is futile. This tendency, which stems from their training, has several sources:

1. Medicine's purpose is to conquer disease. The diagnosis and cure of a disease involve a tremendous personal challenge to a doctor, and success brings great satisfaction.

2. There is a type of vitalism present in the medical profession, going all the way back to the Hippocratic oath, which implies that a physician should always do everything possible to ensure the patient's survival.

3. Because today's laws are unclear, many doctors feel that they have a legal obligation always to treat the patient. They hesitate to act otherwise lest they be prosecuted for manslaughter or malpractice.

4. When incompetent patients suffering from a terminal illness are having the dying process prolonged through life-support measures, many people simply do not know what to do. It is a severe and perplexing problem not only for the family but also for the physicians and health care staff. Even when they recognize the futility of continuing treatment, they hesitate to withdraw treatment already begun. Emotions run

---

[3] Robert Veatch, *Death, Dying and the Biological Revolution, op cit.*, p. 184.

# THREE TYPES OF LIVING WILLS

| Legalizing Active Euthanasia | Clarifying Competent Patients' Rights | Decision-Making For Incompetent Patients |
|---|---|---|
| • voluntary request<br>• person over 21<br>• victim of painful, terminal illness<br>• euthanasia administered under supervision of court or hospital panel<br>• agent not subject to prosecution for homicide | • right to refuse treatments<br>• status of prior requests by now incompetent patient<br>• locus of authority to interpret instructions<br>• question of penalty for not following instructions<br>• deciding on evidence of incompetence with regard to refusal of treatment | • rely on authority of M.D.<br>• rely on authority of next of kin.<br>• rely on authority of guardian.<br>• rely on authority of court. |

very high at such times, and it is difficult to gain a clear perspective on the proper course of action.

For these reasons, many of these bills try to provide a mechanism for determining the wishes of incompetent patients and carrying them out. They try to put the responsibility where it is perceived to belong—on the patient—by ensuring that the person's wishes will be respected even when he or she cannot speak directly to this particular situation.

On the other hand, many argue that such bills are unnecessary and undesirable,[4] for the following reasons:

1. Such wills implicitly affirm that the physician is the correct decision-maker. On the contrary, the individual is the correct decision-maker, and any legislation which attempts to formalize this unwittingly reinforces the popular notion that the physician has the primary authority in this situation.

2. Since the patient already has the right to refuse treatment, such legislation paradoxically serves to undermine that right. For it gives the impression that the patient has been *given* this right by the legislature, whereas in fact he or she already possesses this right in virtue of one's dignity as an individual.

3. If legislation supporting living wills becomes law, what will happen to those who have not made such wills? If incompetent patients have not made such provision, and hence are not covered by the law, they may have to undergo all sorts of treatment that they did not actually desire.

4. Such legislation may be so narrowly drawn that it will fail to cover many actual situations, and thus some of those who might need the law's protection will not in fact be covered by it.

## THE DEBATE GOES ON

The realization is growing that people have the right to refuse any treatment that conflicts with their values and

---

[4] Richard McCormick, S.J. and Andre Hellegers, "Legislation and the Living Will," *America*, March 12, 1977.

desires, and that refusal of such treatment does not constitute *prima facie* evidence of incompetency. This strong affirmation of the right of individuals to determine their own destinies is also having an impact on attitudes toward the rights of incompetent patients.

Two conflicting approaches to medical care converge upon the person who is dying or in a terminal illness and who is also incompetent. On the one hand, there is growing acceptance of the principle that not everything need be done for the dying, especially when nothing is being accomplished except the prolongation of the dying process. On the other hand, new developments in technology and medicine, values inherent in the practice of medicine itself, and genuine respect for the patient make physicians and health care personnel reluctant to abandon treatment of terminal patients.

Legislative initiatives supporting the concept of a living will, while often raising as many problems as they solve, are nevertheless one attempt to address social problems on the level of public policy. If nothing else, discussion about the wisdom of legislating for living wills has served to focus public attention on an urgent issue and perhaps bring its solution a little closer.

### TOPICS FOR DISCUSSION

1. Why has the living will become an issue in our time?

2. After considering the arguments for and against the living will, do you find one side more convincing than the other? If so, which one, and why? If not, why not?

3. Do you think you personally will make a living will? If so, do you have in mind any conditions or limitations that you want spelled out?

### RESOURCES

Annas, George J. "Rights of the Terminally Ill Patient." *Journal of Nursing Administration* 4 (March-April 1974), 40–44.

Aries, Philippe. *Western Attitudes Towards Death: From the Middle Ages to the Present.* Translation by Patricia M. Ranum. Baltimore: John Hopkins University Press, 1974.

Garland, Michael. "The Right To Die in California—Politics, Legislation and Natural Death." Hastings Center *Report* 6 (October 1976), 5–6.

Jonsen, Albert R. "Dying 'Right' in California: The Natural Death Act." *Clinical Research* 26 (February 1978), 55–60.

Lebacqz, Karen. "On Natural Death." Hastings Center *Report* 7 (April 1977), 14.

McCormick, Richard, and Andre Hellegers. "Legislation and the Living Will." *America*, March 12, 1977.

Raible, Jane A. "The Right To Refuse Treatment and Natural Death Legislation." *Medical Legal News* 5 (Fall 1977), 6–8.

Veatch, Robert M. "Death and Dying: The Legislative Options." Hastings Center *Report* 7 (October 1977), 5–8.

*The Right To Die.* Color. 60 mm. 60 minutes. Rent: $55. Sale: $600. Distributor: Macmillan Films, Inc., 34 MacQuesten Parkway South, Mount Vernon, New York 10660.

*Chapter Eight*

---

# NEWBORNS WITH BIRTH DEFECTS

The birth of a child is one of the most profound of all human events. Awe and fascination surround the experience, which is usually the occasion of excitement and joy. The newborn baby can symbolize the parents' mutual love, their hope for the future, and the continuity of the mysterious life process itself. At a moment of such high expectations, the delivery of a child with serious birth defects is a unique and poignant tragedy. Joy and anticipation give way to disappointment and sadness and often to deep feelings of guilt.

Birth defects have aroused varying emotions in different nations and cultures, from horror and revulsion all the way to fascination and reverence.[1] In some times and places such infants have been exterminated; in others, they have been adored. The ancient Babylonians and Egyptians looked on

---

[1] John Fletcher, "Attitudes Towards Defective Newborns," The Hastings Center *Studies* 2:21 (January 1974).

birth defects as signs useful for divination or for predicting good or evil events. Such attitudes spread throughout Europe and influenced attitudes toward such children. Thus, even while they created problems, defective children served significant functions and thus had a place in many ancient cultures.

People have always wondered why such births occur, and for centuries they came up with bizarre explanations founded in superstition. A favorite theory, which has many variations, attributes them to traumas or visions experienced by the mother during pregnancy. We still occasionally hear the folktale that if she sees a rabbit her child will have a harelip. In several European cultures, pregnant women are told to visit museums and to look at works of art so that their children may be born beautiful. There was a time when mothers who gave birth to defective children were suspected of having had intercourse with demons or warlocks or even animals. With the rise of the science of genetics, we now have a better understanding of the causes of birth defects, especially those linked to sex or to the environment of the fetus. We know that if the father or mother has a particular genetic disease, there is a probability that some of their offspring may also suffer from this disease. Recent studies also show that other environmental factors, such as excessive smoking or drinking by the mother, have an impact on the development of the fetus. We are now in a position to understand, more clearly than ever before, how the fetus can be affected by the genetic structure it inherits and the environment in which it develops.

Parents and physicians confront a host of problems when faced with possible or actual birth defects. The most important of these come under four headings: technical, legal, cultural, and ethical.

## THE TECHNICAL DIMENSION

Thanks to the development of a diagnostic process called amniocentesis, it is often possible to tell, long before birth, whether an infant will be abnormal. A long, hollow needle is inserted through the mother's abdomen into the uterus, and a sample is taken of the amniotic fluid in which the fetus is floating. Since this fluid contains fetal cells, these cells can be cultured and tests performed to identify the child's sex and to determine whether it has a particular disease. At present approximately one hundred genetic diseases can be diagnosed *in utero.*

Amniocentesis is usually performed around the fourteenth to sixteenth week of pregnancy, by which time there is enough amniotic fluid to provide a good sample of fetal cells. This can usually be cultured within two or three weeks, but occasionally four to six weeks are required, and sometimes a second tap has to be made. There is no risk to the mother and very little to the fetus—a one or two percent risk of spontaneous abortion, and a very slight possibility of being punctured by the needle. The accuracy rate of diagnosis is about ninety-nine percent,[2] so amniocentesis provides us with a safe and accurate procedure for detecting genetic disease. Unfortunately, it contributes very little to therapy, for although we can diagnose many diseases that the fetus may experience *in utero,* most of these can be treated neither before nor after birth.

This failing creates a curious and ethically disturbing situation. In conventional medicine, diagnosis is aimed at treatment and cure, or at least at improving the patient's condition. But pre-natal diagnosis, while it aims to discover if the fetus will have a birth defect, offers little or no hope of effective treatment. Hence, many assume that the logical conclusion is abortion. Thus the question arises: If you ask for amniocentesis, are you indicating a willingness to resort to abortion? Or, to put the question another way, should amniocentesis be performed only if parents are willing to abort? When we can diagnose a condition but have no way of

---

[2]Charles J. Epstein and Mitchell S. Golbus, "Prenatal Diagnosis of Genetic Diseases," *American Scientist*, November-December, 1977, pp. 307ff.

treating it except eliminating the patient, we face an ethical problem: What should we do with the knowledge that we have gained?

## THE LEGAL DIMENSION

The treatment of babies with birth defects has raised important legal questions. Doctors Raymond Duff and A. G. M. Campbell, in an article in the *New England Journal of Medicine*,[3] described how parents and health care professionals at Yale-New Haven Hospital arrived at joint decisions to allow infants with birth defects to die. Such decisions were made when the prognosis for a meaningful life was hopeless or extremely poor and when further treatment would not cure the condition but simply prolong it. The article concluded with the suggestion that if this was against the law, then the law should be changed.

Among the many responses to this article, one by John Robertson, an attorney, merits detailed consideration. He argues that people may be criminally liable for homicide by omission if they have a legal duty to protect another, if they fail to act despite appropriate knowledge or because of gross negligence, or if the failure to act proximately causes the death of another.[4] Parents have a legal duty to provide necessary medical assistance to a helpless minor child, and case law has generally upheld the homicidal liability of parents whose failure to do so caused the death of a minor child. Thus, child support and providing the necessities of life are required, and maltreatment, cruelty, and endangering the life of a minor child are prohibited. From these facts Robertson concludes that parents who refuse consent to a medical or surgical procedure necessary to maintain the life of an infant with a birth defect or genetic disease are guilty of homicide by omis-

[3]Raymond Duff and A. G. M. Campbell. "Moral and Ethical Dilemmas in the Special Care Nursery," in T. A. Shannon, editor, *Bioethics, op. cit.*, pp. 75ff.

[4]John Robertson. "Involuntary Euthanasia of Defective Newborns: A Legal Analysis," *Stanford Law Review* 27:213.

sion. Moreover, he contends that the attending physician who withholds life-saving treatment from defective infants may be charged with homicide on two separate grounds. First, withholding care or failing to report the case to the proper authorities may violate legal statutes. Second, the knowing or grossly negligent failure to provide care may be the proximate cause of death. Thus, the argument runs, the physician who neglects his or her duty to care for an infant is subject to the charge of involuntary manslaughter.

Robertson forces us to take another look at a widely accepted principle cited in previous chapters of this book: that there is no obligation to provide extraordinary forms of treatment when these do not benefit the patient but simply prolong an illness without curing it. Robertson's legal argument puts this traditional principle of medical ethics in a new light. By focusing on categories of neglect and abuse in evaluating the duties of parents and physicians toward the child, he provides a strong argument against the traditional reliance on the principle of withholding extraordinary or heroic forms of treatment. Many people will be unhappy with Robertson's orientation, but he does force us to rethink the issue from a different perspective. We may have to take into account conditions often ignored in resolving the dilemmas created by children with severe birth defects.

### THE ROLE OF CULTURAL VALUES

A third set of problems in this debate, not always consciously articulated, arises from the cultural values which are at stake in these difficult decisions., There is an understandable tendency to evaluate the infant exclusively in terms of the parents' or the dominant culture's values, and to neglect the infant's intrinsic value and meaning. From this perspective, the child with a birth defect may be seen as almost an insult to the parents and society. Consequently, the real value and interests of the infant are in danger of being ignored or not given their full moral weight.

Sidney Callahan indicates part of the reason for this situation in her book *Parenting*. According to popular expectations, she points out, "parents must produce good, successful children who are healthy, wealthy, wise, and a joy to raise."[5] And for the parents to succeed as good parents, the child must be a perfect child. Obviously, an infant with a birth defect will have trouble meeting any of these standards and is probably a loser from the start, since he or she has destroyed the cultural expectations of the parents and has placed them in an awkward social position. The infant may then be devalued in order to protect the desires of the parents and spare them frustration and social stigma. At any rate, the argument is clearly not child-centered but adult-centered and betrays a hidden bias against the interests of the child.

However, another, more disturbing social force is at work here. We don't like to admit it, but there has been a rather constant American tradition of rejecting and even killing the weak, the helpless, the unwanted, the unacceptable. The Indians, blacks, Orientals, and Chicanos know this from first-hand experience—and there is more than racism involved. The social position of the lower classes has never been an honored or enviable one in this country. In a society that thrives on competition, the less intelligent, the less attractive, and the less aggressive have not had their share of the American dream. In other societies people *suffer* from poverty and weakness; here they are *blamed* for it. It is all too easy to transfer this attitude to the most helpless people of all—infants. Other minority groups can organize, gain political power, and bring their cause to the attention of the public; infants can do none of these things. Perhaps part of the problem, then, is not defective children but a defective society.

## ETHICAL ISSUES

When we approach the problem from an ethical standpoint, we confront four distinct issues: (1) the quality of life; (2)

[5]Sidney Callahan, *Parenting*, Garden City, New York: Doubleday, 1973.

the values involved; (3) the right to make decisions; and (4) the interests of the child.

• *The quality of life.* Those who argue in favor of allowing children with birth defects to die, like those who argue in favor of abortion, base their stand on the importance of the quality of life. Right-to-life groups, which include many Catholics, oppose them and insist on the absolute sacredness of life. In their view, life itself, no matter what the condition, is better than no life at all. The problem with this argument, especially when used by Catholics, is that standard Roman Catholic theology and ethics have often used arguments based on the quality of life. The best example is the doctrine of the just war, first developed by Augustine. He taught that the taking of life was justified in a war against the barbarians who threatened to destroy the civilization of a Roman Empire that had begun to be Christianized. This was a far cry from the earlier world-rejecting stance of persecuted Christians who gladly and even eagerly sought martyrdom in order to enter into the fullness of glory. Now it was better to be a citizen in an empire that protected Christianity and civilization than to be a slave of barbarians who could only destroy what was worthwhile.

This was the first but not the last time that the quality-of-life argument influenced Christian theology. After centuries of condemning usury, the practice of charging interest on loans, the Church finally accepted it in medieval times and thus implicitly blessed the new money economy which replaced the feudal system. An almost absolute prohibition of usury was abandoned because of what banking and money could do for Europe and, implicitly, the Church. Even if one does not accept this interpretation of that shift in doctrine, it must be admitted that the acceptance of usury represented a significant and instructive theological compromise with the socio-economic forces of the Middle Ages.

A more recent example is the teaching of modern popes about the workers' right to a living wage. In the encyclicals *Rerum Novarum, Quadragesimo Anno,* and *Mater et Magistra,* they insist that the employer's right to profits is qualified by the right of workers and their families to a decent life and a certain standard of living, including the ability to make some provision for the future.

Finally, the papal approval of periodic continence or "rhythm" as a form of birth control is another example of the quality-of-life argument. Couples may restrict relations to the "natural" sterile period to avoid having children for reasons of health, economics, or education. If the mother would suffer prolonged illness, or if the family did not have the resources to care for their children, or if they could not provide for their proper education, then the use of rhythm was morally acceptable. This very clearly says that a certain quality of life is important for the family and the child-to-be.

## CHURCH TEACHING AND
## THE QUALITY OF LIFE ARGUMENT

| CHURCH TEACHING | QUALITY OF LIFE ARGUMENT |
|---|---|
| Just War | Taking of life justified to preserve society |
| Acceptance of Usury | Banking and money needed for growth of social system |
| Workers' Right to Just Wage | Right of employer to profit is qualified by workers' right to decent life |
| Approval of Rhythm Method of Birth Control | Procreation may be restricted for medical, economic and educational reasons |

Along the spectrum of reactions to the quality-of-life argument, two extreme positions emerge: a complete rejection of it by ignoring its existence, and the use of it to justify almost anything. The more serious reaction is the total ignoring of this argument, especially by Roman Catholics. By refusing to give it any weight, we implicitly reject major theological developments in our tradition, while calmly accepting their conclusions. This kind of inconsistency was painfully evident during most of the Vietnam War when many in the American

Church used the quality-of-life argument to justify a savage military campaign abroad while turning a deaf ear to such considerations in the abortion debate at home. If we are to be honest about tradition and theological developments, we must recognize the fact that quality of life has had an honored, though selectively applied, place in that tradition. In doing so, we would not inevitably agree to every use of that argument, for other considerations can and should be raised. However, we could admit, for example, that those who use this argument in the debate about birth defects are not automatically outside the Roman Catholic tradition. This would provide a clear and honest starting point from which to engage in the debate. Then we can either use the argument, recognizing it as part of traditional Catholic ethical theory, or we can reject it, realizing that in so doing we would revert to the very earliest traditions of the Church.

• *The values involved.* A second ethical issue concerns the values on which we base decisions concerning infants with birth defects. The families of such children bring to the situation sets of values which are more or less conscious at the outset and which become more prominent as it develops. In a traumatic context, they are under severe pressure to make some kind of decision. They may not know how to express their value preferences, and they may even be ashamed to do so, but it is important for them to deal with their feelings and to face honestly the consequences of the choices open to them.

Health care personnel, too, have their own values and preferences. As professionals, they also have duties and obligations. These personal values and professional obligations are often in harmony, but sometimes they conflict. Physicians are trained to combat disease and illness and to do everything they can to cure them. Other health care professionals are trained to do specific tasks and find it difficult to refrain from doing them. Both these groups are accustomed to working within limited spheres of competence and may not be equipped to deal with larger, more comprehensive issues. Like the rest of us, they may or may not be skillful in relating to people caught up in grief and tragedy. Such limitations are not necessarily personal failings, but they do make it difficult to come to grips with urgent human problems. As a result, questions of value may never be clearly formulated, and people may unconsciously find ways to avoid issues instead of facing them.

• *Who should decide?* Should the doctor make the final decision, or the parents? Doctors have expertise in diagnosis and treatment and are qualified to make medical judgments, but they may not be equipped to judge in this particular case. Moreover, the technical qualifications to make medical judgments are not the same as the ability to make value judgments. And if the physician and the parents have different values, they will have different perceptions and will come up with different solutions. It is to the parents that the child belongs, though not in the same way as property belongs to them. They are the ones who have the primary responsibility to care for the child. It is their life-style and quality of life that will be affected, and their values that will be put to the test. As such, they may be the ones who are entitled to make decisions in these cases.

• *The interests of the child.* If decisions are to be made in an ethically responsible manner, then the interests not only of the family but also of the child must be respected.[6] But what *are* the interests of the child, and how do we determine them? There are at least three ways we might proceed, none of them completely satisfactory. First, we could equate a child's interests with what a competent adult ought to do in similar circumstances. For example, we say that a morally responsible person ought to make some sacrifices for the community. Does this include an obligation to make the supreme sacrifice of

---

[6]Normand Fost, "Proxy Consent for Seriously Ill Newborns," *No Rush to Judgment*, Volume 1, David H. Smith, editor, The Poynter Center: Indiana University, 1977.

dying for one's family or community? Second, we might equate children's interests with their expressed desires, if they are capable of such expression. With an infant this is obviously impossible. And even if a child is able to express his or her wishes, should we give to those wishes the same respect that we give to an adult's? Third, we could use the process known as substitute judgment. Here a decision is made on the basis of what a competent person would do if placed in the child's situation. This seems a valid approach, but it has its problems. How can I project my values into a situation and an organism which I am incapable of experiencing? On the other hand, someone must make a decision. And a substitute decision by the proper decision-maker, for example the parents, might come as close as anything yet known to expressing the best interests of the child.

• *The interests of the child may be equated with:* What a competent adult would do in a similar situation *or*: The expressed desires of the child *or*: The judgment of a competent person who puts himself or herself in the child's place.

An infant with birth defects presents parents and physicians with many serious and difficult questions of value. Before they can make decisions, they must examine not only a great deal of technical and diagnostic material, but also their own values and the surrounding cultural attitudes toward such children. Even when they have done all these things, they may still find the decision hard to make and harder to live with. However, decide they must, and reasonably soon, so that treatment may be begun or ended before the child is placed in a kind of medical holding pattern.

Four distinct options are available if we decide to formulate and enact a public policy for decision-making.[7] 1. Parents and physicians could legally be given broad discretionary powers to treat or withhold treatment from newborns with birth defects. Society would trust them to make the critical

[7]John Robertson, *loc. cit.*

choices. 2. The right to withhold treatment could be limited to specific classes of defects. 3. An impartial third party, such as a court or a review committee, would be empowered to decide on treatment or non-treatment. 4. We could maintain the present system, which informally delegates decision-making powers to parents and physicians, rather than giving them any explicit legal credentials.

None of these policies will spare people the inevitable anxiety connected with such situations, but they would at least put the decision-making process on a formal basis and lessen the anguish to some degree. This kind of formalization of procedures may help us to clarify the values involved and to make choices that are painful but sound.

## TOPICS FOR DISCUSSION

1. If you or your wife were expecting a child in about six months, and the doctor asked if you wished to undergo amniocentesis, what would you say? Why?

2. In the controversy between Doctors Duff and Campbell and Attorney John Robertson, who do you feel makes more sense? Does your answer give you a clearer insight into your underlying moral premises and values?

3. What new light does Robertson throw on the traditional moral principle that distinguishes between ordinary and extraordinary treatment?

4. What do the authors mean when they say that part of the problem may be not defective children but a defective society?

5. "In other societies people *suffer* from poverty and weakness; here [in America] they are *blamed* for it." Explain this statement. Do you agree with it?

6. During the divisive era of the Vietnam War, many of the pro-abortionists were against the war, and many of the anti-abortionists supported the war. How do you explain these paradoxes?

7. Rank the four options for decision-making at the very end of the chapter in the order of your personal preference. Give reasons for your choices.

## RESOURCES

Duff, Raymond S., and A. G. M. Campbell. "Moral and Ethical Dilemmas in the Special-Care Nursery." *New England Journal of Medicine* 289 (October 25, 1973) 890–94.

Fletcher, John C. "Abortion, Euthanasia and Care of Defective Newborns." *New England Journal of Medicine* 292 (January 9, 1975), 75–78.

Gustafson, James M. "Mongolism, Parental Desires and the Right to Life." *Perspectives in Biology and Medicine* 16 (Summer 1973), 529–57.

Jonsen, A. R., and Michael Garland, editors. *Ethics of Newborn Intensive Care.* San Francisco and Berkeley: University of California School of Medicine and Institute of Governmental Studies, 1976.

McCormick, Richard A. "To Save or Let Die: The Dilemma of Modern Medicine." *Journal* of the American Medical Association 229 (July 8, 1974), 172–76.

Robertson, John A. "Involuntary Euthanasia of Defective Newborns: A Legal Analysis." *Stanford Law Review* 27 (January 1975), 213–67.

Shaw, Anthony. "Dilemmas of 'Informed Consent' in Children." *New England Journal of Medicine* 289 (October 25, 1973), 885–90.

Swinyard, Chester A., editor. *Decision-Making and the Defective Newborn.* Springfield, Illinois: Charles C. Thomas, Publisher, 1977.

Weber, Leonard J. *Who Shall Live? The Dilemma of Severely Handicapped Children and Its Meaning for Other Moral Questions.* New York: Paulist Press, 1976.

Zachary, R. B. "Life with Spina Bifida." *British Medical Journal*, December 9, 1977, pp. 1460–62.

*A Question of Values.* Color. 16 mm. 24 minutes. Rent $15. Sale $125. Distributor: Mental Development Center, Case Western Reserve University, Cleveland, Ohio 44106.

*Who Should Survive?* Color. 16 mm. 26 minutes. Rent $20. Sale $150. Distributor: Patricia Furman, 209 East Broad St., Falls Church, Virginia 22046.

*Spina Bifida with Meningomyelocele: Should We Operate?* Black and white. 3/4″ videocassette. 60 minutes. Sale $68. Distributor: Dr. Bernard Towers, Department of Pediatrics, School of Medicine, U.C.L.A., Los Angeles, Calif. 90024.

*Chapter Nine*

---

# ORGAN TRANSPLANTS

The Six Million Dollar Man and the Bionic Woman are two television characters who inhabit the shadow world of science fiction, somewhere between fact and fantasy. They would be products of pure imagination were it not for the fact that organ transplants and the development of artificial organs and limbs are now an accepted fact of life. Our capacity to produce artificial hips, arms, hands, and knees and to exchange corneas and kidneys no longer makes headlines. Pacemakers, which help the heart to maintain a constant beat, are a familiar part of the medical landscape. The next big story will be the totally implantable artificial heart, which is being developed at the National Heart and Lung Institutes and is at the stage of animal experimentation. This growing ability to shuffle and exchange vital body parts among human beings makes it possible not only to preserve life but to improve its quality. It also brings with it many difficult moral problems that call for solution.

To be sure, progress in transplanting is neither easy, nor cheap, nor complete. The tendency of the host body to reject the transplanted organ is still a major problem that is yielding slowly to advancement in surgical techniques. The cost of medical care and hospitalization involved in these operations is extremely high. And we have not yet faced the question dramatized by Six Million Dollar Man: Should we be content with normal functioning of artificial and transplanted organs, or should we seek maximum efficiency for these organs, so that individuals will be better qualified for performing certain tasks? Nevertheless, we are making progress and will continue to do so. This chapter examines some of the consequences of the new situation.

The major ethical questions are these:

- Is transplanting justifiable, and under what conditions?
- Who shall benefit, and how shall we choose those who are to be helped?
- Who has the right to donate organs, for themselves and for others?
- From whom may organs rightly be taken?
- Where and how can we obtain organs for those who need them?

Let us now examine these questions and the problems they involve.

- *Can we justify transplants?* This problem concerns the donor's bodily integrity: Is it right for us to dispose of the members and functions of our bodies? Traditional Roman Catholic theology said yes, provided that the principle of totality was observed. This principle allowed amputations, for instance, so long as such a mutilation was required for the good of the whole of that particular person. But how could I justify donating my organs to someone else? Not only does my body not benefit, but it seems to be deprived. The solution was found when we realized that the human body in many instances has dual organs and can function almost as well with one as with two. Kidneys are one such case, but not the only one. Therefore Catholic theologians approved organ transplantations as a response to the Lord's command to love and care for one another. Rather than simply depriving our bodies of some member or function, we would be taking a reasonable risk in order to help our neighbor.

• *Under what conditions may we proceed?* James Nelson[1] lays down five criteria by which we may judge the legitimacy of a particular organ transplantation. First, transplantation should be the last resort. This means that no other treatment will be as effective, and there must be a reasonable hope that the transplantation will be successful. Second, the primary intent must be the patient's welfare, not simply an experiment to improve the state of medical knowledge. The advancement of medical science is a legitimate aim, but restoring the patient to health comes first. To put it crudely, people may not be substituted for guinea pigs. Third, there must be free consent. The patient must be informed of the physical and psychological risks involved in the operation and, in the light of this knowledge, freely give permission to proceed.

Nelson's fourth criterion is the protection of the innocent—the patient and the family and the donor. In helping the patient and the family to make the decision, medical personnel should not raise false hopes by promising more than the operation can deliver. And those concerned should consider whether the operation constitutes an ordinary or an extraordinary means of treatment, and hence whether it is obligatory or not. The rights of the donor, too, must be respected, though this can be very difficult in practice. If the donor is dying, physicians must resist the temptation to subject the individual to prolonged, painful treatment and needless suffering just to make sure that they obtain a healthy organ. In this case, too much treatment would violate the donor's rights. At the other extreme, they must avoid doing too little for this person. In this situation, a donor could be declared dead even though

[1]James Nelson, *Human Medicine, op. cit.*, pp. 152ff.

beneficial treatment might still be possible. Or they might neglect to notify relatives or next of kin to get consent to stop treatment. The motive—to obtain the needed organ—would be good, but the rights of the donor would be violated. The fifth and last criterion is that of proportionality. Will the patient receive enough benefit to outweigh the cost of the treatment? Transplantation procedures are extremely expensive, and there must be some proportion between the results obtained and the financial hardships endured.

• *Who is to benefit, and how do we decide?* The problem here is one of supply and demand. More and more people need treatment, but organs and other resources are scarce. There are not nearly enough dialysis machines available to care for all the people with kidney failure. Not enough people voluntarily donate their organs to others either while living or after their death. So how do we decide who gets what and when? Three solutions are proposed: the social worth system, random selection, and triage.

In the so-called *social worth* system, the people selected for treatment will be those who have made or probably will continue to make valuable contributions to society. This could mean, for example, that a physician may be regarded as more socially valuable than a garbage collector. In deciding people's qualifications to receive a scarce life-saving resource, they would be considered in terms of the way society ranks certain values and occupations. *Random selection*, on the other hand, may take one of two forms. The natural type is based on a principle such as first come, first served. The artificial form might be a lottery system. The purpose of such procedures would be to preserve human dignity by being fair and providing equal opportunity for all who need scarce life-saving resources. Finally, there is the approach called *triage*. This system, based on the French word *trier*, "to sort," developed during medical emergencies on the battlefield. The wounded were sorted into three groups. The first would die no matter what care they received. The second would recover even if untreated. The undermanned medics ignored these and treated the third group, who would survive only if cared for immediately. Such a method concentrates resources and energy on those who have a chance to survive if treated, and implies that patients in the other two groups will not receive treatment that they may need.

• *Who should be the donors?* It is important that those who donate organs do so freely. If the person is not yet of age, or if he or she realizes how critical is the patient's dependence, there will be strong pressure, and voluntary consent will be inhibited. However, as long as it is not clear that consent is uninformed or unfree, we should be careful not to prevent people from making decisions they are entitled to make. The problem of consent arises in a different form when the potential donor is unconscious or dying. (This is why people are encouraged to donate their organs in writing beforehand; one of the author's brothers, before his death, willed his eyes to whoever might need them.) In such a case, who is to give consent? Often the next of kin does so; sometimes the court may make a decision, especially if the person has previously been deemed mentally incompetent.

The case of the dying donor becomes even more complex when we consider the definition of death. Depending on how we define death, a physician is open to charges of homicide or manslaughter for removing organs prematurely. Perhaps we should revise the definition of death so that more fresh organs for implantation might be available. If brain death is the criterion, rather than lung or heart failure, we can maintain the circulation of blood and oxygen in the dead person's body so that the organs may be preserved until actually needed. We would then have a legally dead cadaver which would be warm, breathing, and excreting, and which would require feeding and grooming. Such a bio-mort, as described, by Willard Gaylin,[2] could probably be maintained for at least a year. It would provide major organs, such as kidneys, heart, and possibly lungs for transplantations, as well as arteries and skin. Its

[2]Willard Gaylin, "Harvesting the Dead," in T. A. Shannon, editor, *Bioethics, op. cit.*, pp. 413ff.

blood would be a continual source for transfusion. Medical instructors could use it to teach physicians how to treat a patient and how to perform surgery, and for various experiments. Since the person is legally dead, there is no need for consent and no question of homicide.

• *Where and how can we obtain organs?* As medicine and science continue to take giant steps of progress, organ transplants become easier and more routine. Still, the organs are always in critically short supply, so that we have the skill but not the materials to help people in desperate need. In some states there is a space on drivers' licenses where one can indicate that he or she is willing to donate organs for transplantation. This is a beautiful way to show that we love one another. In donating organs from my body, I recognize that others may deed what I no longer need. I go beyond my own personal concerns and express solidarity with other members of the human family. In a dramatic way I offer to another the most precious gift of life.

This dimension of organ transplantation is important to remember, for there are other aspects that may be distasteful, and even gruesome. Some of the transplantation scenarios are ghastly, and some science fiction fantasies, especially with regard to bionics, are repugnant. Still, it is hard to imagine a more practical way to have an impact on the life and survival rate of another person. Volunteering to be the donor of an organ involves us in the lives of others, shows them that we care, and contributes effectively to the quality of life, and even to life itself.

## TOPICS FOR DISCUSSION

The following two cases[3] are the true stories of people who needed transplants, of their potential donors, and of the decisions which had to be made by a judge and a doctor.

1. One of two eight-year-old girls, identical twins, suffers

---

[3]Robert Veach, *op. cit.*, pp. 223ff. and pp. 225ff.

from a serious kidney disease, hemolytic uremic syndrome, and has to have both kidneys removed. The only available donor who presents a high probability of successful transplantation is her twin sister. The parents are too agitated to make the decision, and they have the court appoint an independent guardian who talks with the child and becomes convinced that she understands to the limit of her age and wants to help. A psychiatrist agrees that she is not subject to undue pressure.

Should the judge permit the parents to approve the transplant? It would be of immense benefit to the sick twin, but presents some risk and limited benefit to the donor. The child herself is not legally competent to give consent.

2. A middle-aged woman suffering from chronic renal disease has two choices: either a kidney transplant or dialysis. She strongly prefers a transplant, since dialysis involves spending six hours a day, three days a week, attached to a dialysis machine, for the rest of her life.

The only donor with a good chance of success is her sister, who has indicated a willingness to donate one of her kidneys. Her husband, however, is opposed. He points out to the doctor that his wife leads an active life, has several young children to care for, and is deeply involved in other activities of a professional nature. She also has some medical problems. His sister-in-law, on the other hand, lives a sedentary life and can do quite well on dialysis. Moreover, he is convinced that his wife does not really want to donate the organ but does not know how to refuse her sister.

The doctor, after conferring with her and enlisting the aid of a psychiatrist, seriously doubts that she is willing to give the kidney freely.

After obtaining the tissue-typing, which indicates an ideal match, the doctor has four alternatives. Which should he choose?

(a) Tell her of the good match.

(b) Tell her of the good match, but offer to tell the sick sister that the match is not acceptable.

(c) Tell her the match is unacceptable.

(d) Tell her the match is good, but refuse to perform the transplant because he is not convinced that she is willing to give the organ freely.

## RESOURCES

Eastwood, R. T., *et al. Cardiac Replacement: Medical, Ethical, Psychological and Economic Implications.* A Report by the Ad Hoc Task Force on Cardiac Replacement, National Heart Institute, National Institutes of Health. Washington, D.C.: U.S. Government Printing Office, 1969.

Fox, Renee C., and Judith P. Swazey. *The Courage To Fail: A Social View of Organ Transplants and Dialysis.* Chicago: University of Chicago Press, 1974.

Katz, Jay, and Alexander M. Capron. *Catastrophic Diseases: Who Decides What? A Psychological and Legal Analysis of the Problems Posed by Hemodialysis and Organ Transplantation.* New York: Russell Sage Foundation, 1975.

Levy, Normand B., editor. *Living or Dying: Adaptation to Hemodialysis.* Springfield, Illinois: Charles C. Thomas, Publisher, 1974.

Lyons, Catherine. *Organ Transplants: The Moral Issues.* Philadelphia: The Westminster Press, 1970.

Titmuss, Richard P. *The Gift Relationship: From Human Blood to Social Policy.* New York: Pantheon Books, 1971.

"The Totally Implantable Artificial Heart." A Report by the Artificial Heart Assessment Panel, National Heart and Lung Institute, June 1973. National Heart and Lung Institute, National Institutes of Health, Bethesda, Maryland.

Wolstenholm, E. W., and Maeve O'Connor, editors. *Epics in Medical Progress: With Special Reference to Transplantation.* Boston: Little, Brown and Company, 1975.

*Dialysis Procedures.* Color. 16mm. 27 minutes. Rent: Free. Distributor: Eli Lilly and Company, Audiovisual Film Library, Department MC 340, Indianapolis, Indiana.

*Gift of Life/Right To Die.* Black and white. 16 mm. 16 minutes. Rent: $4.40. Distributor: Visual Aids Service, Division University Extension, University of Illinois, Champagne, Illinois 61822.

*Heart Makers.* Color. 16mm. 15 minutes. Rent: $20.50. Sale: $550. Distributor: Indiana University Audiovisual Center, Bloomington, Indiana 47401.

*Kidney Failure and Hemodialysis: Should Everyone Be Treated?* Black and white. 3/4" videocassette. 60 minutes. Sale: $68. Distributor: Dr. Bernard Towers, Department of Pediatrics, School of Medicine, U.C.L.A., Los Angeles, Calif. 90024.

# Chapter Ten

---

# RESEARCH INVOLVING HUMAN SUBJECTS

The Panama Canal almost didn't get built, and you could have blamed it on the mosquitos. At one time the project was abandoned because, among other reasons, workmen by the thousands were dying of yellow fever. No one was sure how the disease was being transmitted, but one man thought it might be from mosquito bites. The only way to find out was to use human subjects, so people volunteered to expose themselves to the disease and possible death, the fate of one of the physician-researchers. Because of their research, it was learned that mosquitos carried the disease. When their breeding grounds were destroyed, yellow fever was eliminated and the Panama Canal became a reality.

Everyone rejoices when new medical discoveries take place. A cure for a previously hopeless disease or a new, less expensive, or more effective treatment for serious ailments is hailed as a breakthrough, and the discoverers are nominated for Nobel Prizes. We admire and respect the dedicated researchers who make these breakthroughs, for we know that years of painstaking study and experimentation were required. When they succeed, we rightly hail them as benefactors of humankind. We are all waiting for a breakthrough in the search for a cure for cancer, for muscular dystrophy, and for the common cold.

These discoveries would probably happen more often and much sooner if researchers could use human subjects instead of animals and lower forms of life. The basic moral objection, however, is clear: the purpose of experimentation is not to help *this* patient, but to advance medical knowledge so that future patients may be healed. Hence, the physician would in effect be treating this patient not as an end but as a means. And a most important human value—respect for the worth of the individual person—would be lost. Thus medical researchers are often forced to limit themselves in their work, using animals and coming up with data and results that are never quite satisfactory. For no one knows if this treatment will work where it really counts—with real live people. What cures mice doesn't always cure people.

How can we bridge this gap? The obvious way is to obtain permission from the individuals who are to be the subjects of research. If their consent is free and informed, the reasoning goes, there would be no question of using or taking advantage of people, since it would be their own decision. However, a major ethical debate now centers on this point. Some people say that obtaining genuinely free consent is impossible; others say that it is both possible and desirable and that the government is already involved in regulating the procedure. The National Commission for the Protection of Human Subjects of Biomedical and Behavioral Research, in existence for four years, developed many recommendations for protecting the rights of human subjects.

Many individuals argue that informed consent cannot be obtained. They give four reasons. First, people are always impressed by doctors and scientists who become authority figures for them and are psychologically very hard to refuse. In such circumstances, "free" consent is not really free. Second, if subjects were told of all the possible risks involved in the experiment, they would be too afraid to go ahead. This creates a dilemma for researchers: if they don't level with their patients, they will be dishonest and unjust; if they do tell all, they may not have anyone to experiment on. Third, most medical experiments are too complicated to explain to the patients; the latter cannot give real consent to something they don't even understand. Fourth, the patient is not the only one who suffers from ignorance. Even the researcher does not know all the things that can happen; if these were clear, we wouldn't need the experiment in the first place. So investigators cannot obtain properly informed consent, since they are not that informed themselves. In spite of these problems, many feel that we should go ahead anyway with the experimentation and research, since these will do so much good; they would put less emphasis on obtaining informed consent.

## INFORMED CONSENT

Others, however, feel that there are many reasons to obtain such consent. People, after all, have the right to choose their own values and to make decisions based on those values. They are entitled to form their own opinions and to make up their minds on the basis of available evidence. If we respect the individual and are determined to treat persons as ends and not as means, we will not manipulate them or use them for any purpose, however noble. Giving them maximum information and freedom to choose protects their autonomy and respects their dignity. Moreover, requiring informed consent is a way of protecting people whose autonomy is limited, such as minors, mental patients, and prisoners. People who cannot protect themselves should be protected by society. In some of these cases substitute consent, by persons such as relatives or guardians, could be obtained to allow them to participate in experimentation and research.

Into this controversy has stepped the federal government,

in the form of guidelines issued by the Department of Health, Education, and Welfare. These guidelines define informed consent as "the knowing consent of an individual or his or her legally authorized representative, so situated as to be able to exercise free power of choice without undue inducement or any element of force, fraud, deceit, duress, or other form of constraint or coercion."[1] They then spell out the information that must be given: (1) explain the procedures and their purposes, and make clear which are experimental; (2) spell out the risks and discomforts that can be reasonably expected; (3) describe the possible benefits expected; (4) point out appropriate alternatives that might help the subject; (5) offer to answer any questions about the procedures; (6) make it clear to the subject that he or she is free without penalty to withdraw consent and abandon the project at any time.

These requirements and safeguards will not solve all the problems described above with regard to free consent, but they do protect some basic values that are at stake in this matter. They serve to give individuals the information needed to make prudent and free decisions about participating in experimentation and research. They help to insure that people will not be used, and that their dignity as persons will be respected and preserved.

## SELECTION OF SUBJECTS

Human experiments raise another question: How do we select people to experiment on? Four different ways[2] have been suggested. (1) Select the best educated, most highly motivated members of society available. The ideal subject would be a scientist-researcher, since he or she is best qualified to understand what is happening and to report accurately the results and findings of the experiment. This kind of self-experimentation takes place from time to time, but not in

---

[1] 45CFR 46:103. 11 January 1978.

[2] Hans Jonas, "Reflections on Experimenting with Human Subjects," in T. A. Shannon, *Bioethics, op. cit.*, pp. 222ff.

great numbers. (2) Take the marginal people from outside the mainstream of society—the poor, prisoners, the defenseless, those on welfare—who are most expendable. There is a tradition of using the poor this way, sometimes offering treatment in exchange for agreement to participate in experiments. (3) Take those who are willing to sell their services. The only qualification would be that the price is right. This method of selection has been used fairly often in the past. (4) Choose the subjects from the entire population by lot, the way soldiers have been conscripted through the Selective Service lottery. Since the entire population benefits from scientific and medical research, everyone would have an equal chance of bearing the burden and the risks. There is no precedent for anything like this, and it would probably meet with great resistance from the public. Yet the shortage of subjects is critical, and we perhaps too easily assume that the benefits of medical progress will continue without our paying the price involved in experimentation.

Assuming that subjects have been chosen for research, that they have freely consented and that their rights have been safeguarded, we are left with one ethical question: How can such participation be justified? Do we have the right to take such chances with our bodies, and even with our lives?

## JUSTIFYING RESEARCH

A variety of arguments has been advanced to justify these risks.[3] One is the social contract theory, which sees them as a way the individual repays society for benefits received from past research. We all profit from medical progress that resulted from sacrifices made by others in the past; it is only right that we should make a similar contribution now for the sake of those who come after us. A second form of justification is the theory of self-sacrifice. In this case one does not think about the benefits received for oneself, but simply about the

[3]*Ibid.*, pp. 213ff.

needs of others. Whether or not I receive anything in return is unimportant; what matters is how I can contribute to the welfare of others, even at a cost to myself. In terms of Christian idealism, this reflects the teaching of Jesus: "Greater love than this no man has, that he lay down his life for his friends."

A third theory justifying participation in research stresses the utilitarian principle: I have a general obligation to participate because of the goods that it will bring to myself and to others, for research advances scientific knowledge, which is seen as the highest value in our society, and which benefits everyone. This theory focuses on only one primary value—knowledge for its own sake—and suggests that every member of society should contribute to the attainment of this value in some way. My fate is tied up with the fate of others, and the goods that I pursue may be good for others as well. Thus, in working for my own social good, I am also working for the social good of others. We can thus argue that individuals have a social obligation to participate in experiments, because such participation brings about human growth and well-being.

There is no denying the fact that scientists and doctors have sometimes engaged in highly unethical experiments. Some of these have been well publicized and have given research a bad image in the minds of many. This is unfortunate, because many ethical projects, carried out by researchers sensitive to the rights of subjects and patients, have done a great deal of good. They could do even more if enough people would participate in some of the highly ethical and well-designed research protocols that are available. These contracts, entered into by persons who wish to contribute to medical and scientific progress, are a splendid way to make a meaningful contribution to society. From a religious point of view, it is a specific, concrete way to put into practice the great commandment to love one another. Taking part in a research protocol should be considered seriously by those who sincerely want to fulfill their civic and social obligations and to express concern for their companions in society.

## TOPICS FOR DISCUSSION

1. Discuss the issue of *consent*. Why is it so important in medical research and experiments? What are some of the circumstances that make it difficult to obtain? Why are researchers sometimes tempted to dispense with it?

2. Participating in experiments often involves serious danger to oneself. What considerations are offered as justification?

3. An oral contraceptive manufacturer and a federal agency wanted to find out if the reported side-effects were due to physiological or merely psychological causes. The subjects were mostly poor Mexican-American women who had had at least two children and had come to a San Antonio clinic for birth control assistance. They all thought they were receiving contraceptives, but seventy-six of them received only dummy pills, though all were told to use a vaginal cream as well in case the pill didn't work. Ten of them became pregnant during the course of the experiment.[4] Was this procedure ethical?

4. The 5,200 mentally retarded children at Willowbrook State Hospital in Staten Island, New York, were very vulnerable to such diseases as hepatitis, measles, shigellosis, and parasitic and respiratory infections. In order to understand and develop a method of immunization against hepatitis, researchers injected infected serum in over seven hundred children to produce hepatitis. They justified their decision on the following grounds: (a) the children were exposed to the virus just by being at the institution; (b) they were lodged in a specially equipped unit where they were isolated from exposure to the other prevalent diseases; (c) they were likely to have a sub-clinical infection followed by immunity to hepatitis; and (d) the consent of the parents was obtained beforehand.

A nationally-known surgeon commented on the case: "There was a tremendous uproar over the ethical approach,

[4]Hasings Center *Report*, 1:2 (June 1971).

but the results were fantastic, and couldn't have been obtained any other way."[5]

Discuss the ethics of this experiment.

## RESOURCES

Annas, George J., Leonard H. Glanz, and Barbara F. Katz. *Informed Consent to Human Experimentation: The Subject's Dilemma* Cambridge: The Ballinger Publishing Company, 1977.

Barber, Bernard, *et al. Research on Human Subjects: Problems of Social Control in Medical Experimentation.* New York: Russell Sage Foundation, 1973.

Beecher, Henry K. *Research in the Individual: Human Studies.* Boston: Little, Brown and Company, 1970.

*Experiments and Research with Humans: Values in Conflict.* Washington, D.C.: National Academy of Sciences, 1975.

Katz, J., editor, with Alexander M. Capron and Eleanor Swiftglass. *Experimentation with Human Beings.* New York: Russell Sage Foundation, 1972.

Rivlin, Alice M., and P. Michael Timpane, editors. *Ethical and Legal Issues of Social Experimentation.* Washington, D.C.: The Brookings Institution, 1975.

Visscher, Maurice B. *Ethical Constraints and Imperatives in Medical Research.* Springfield, Illinois: Charles C. Thomas, Publisher, 1975.

*The Ultimate Experimental Animal: Man.* Color. 16mm. 37 minutes. Rent: $19. Sale: $400. Distributor: Films, Inc., 1144 Wilmette Ave., Wilmette, Illinois 60091.

*Ethical Problems in Medical Research.* Color. Videotape. 26 minutes. Distributor: University of Texas Medical School at San Antonio, Department of Medical Communications Research, San Antonio, Texas.

*Informed Consent: Is It Possible or Even Always Desirable?*

[5]Jay Katz, *Experimentation with Human Beings*, New York: Russell Sage Foundation, 1972, pp. 1008ff.

Black and white. 3/4″ videocassette. 60 minutes. Sale: $68. Distributor: Dr. Bernard Towers, Department of Pediatrics, School of Medicine, U.C.L.A., Los Angeles, Calif. 90024.

*The Science and Ethics of Human Drug Trials: Problems and Solutions.* Black and white. 16 mm. 60 minutes. Distributor: Media Resources Branch, National Medical Audiovisual Center, Station K, Atlanta, Georgia 30324.

*Chapter Eleven*

---

# BEHAVIOR MODIFICATION

Two of the most powerful and influential movies of the 1970's were *A Clockwork Orange* and *One Flew Over the Cuckoo's Nest*. In the former, a violent young criminal is subjected to behavior conditioning that turns him into a passive personality unable to deal even with normal aggression. In the latter, the bad guys are the doctors and nurses in an insane asylum. They use behavioral control methods, including radical brain surgery like pre-frontal labotomy, to render patients manageable, but in the process they destroy them as human beings.

These films dramatized the fears of many people about a branch of science sometimes described as "behavior technology" and run by those whom Vance Packard calls "people shapers." Senator Edward Kennedy, chairman of the Senate Subcommittee on Health, believes that uncontrolled people-shaping will make bioethics the frontier of constitutional law for the rest of this century.

When we hear of behavior modification we think of brain-washing, and that reminds us of Korea, Vietnam, and some religious cults. The Korean War introduced Americans to the enormous power of brainwashing techniques when captured servicemen were programmed to denounce the United States. Some of the Vietnam War veterans who turned against America seem to have been influenced by mind-control techniques. We have come to realize how easily these methods can change a person's ideas, beliefs, and loyalties. Therefore when young followers of some extremist cult give up their former beliefs and life-style and offer total, unconditional loyalty, it looks like another case of mass brainwashing. Ironically, some of these youngsters' parents are now kidnaping them and "deprogramming" them in a kind of reverse mind-control process. Thus both sides in the struggle seem to disagree on all but one thing—the use of behavior modification principles.

## EVERYDAY FORMS

To put this issue in perspective, consider some areas in our ordinary lives where behavior modification has always gone on and has been taken for granted. Two of the most obvious examples are toilet training and teaching table manners to children. We don't ordinarily think of these in such sophisticated terms, but what is happening? The behavior of individuals is being modified, in the interest of hygiene and aesthetics, for the benefit of other members of society.

Education is another part of our lives where behavior modification is an implicit part of the social system. From nursery school to graduate school, teachers and administrators are trying to modify students' behavior. School is just one part of the whole process of socialization, whereby people are groomed to take their position and play their role in society. In the process, a variety of pressures are brought upon students to help them achieve entry into, say, a certain profession. However, the individual is not supposed to remain passive, but to take an active role in evaluating the profession, his or her own interests, and the process of education itself. This creates certain contradictory tensions among educators. Is schooling supposed to equip people to fill prescribed roles in the prevailing scheme of things, or should it free people to challenge the prevailing order and change it? How much self-criticism can a society stand? You can find teachers at all points of the spectrum, from those who see education as indoctrination all the way to those who consider it a legitimately subversive activity. The indoctrinators are obviously in the behavior modification business.

The young and the weak are not the only ones who experience these pressures. We usually think of political officeholders as powerful and influential people, and they often are, but they are also subject to many subtle forms of manipulation. Status symbols connected with an office influence the way one relates to the job. It's hard to think of yourself as the servant of the people while traveling first class, accompanied by a corps of secretaries, and being driven in a chauffeured limousine. The political process itself, featuring lobbyists, wealthy campaign contributors, ethnic voting blocs, and wheeling and dealing in smoke-filled rooms, exerts tremendous pressure on politicians and makes them some of the least free people in a democratic society. If one of them perceives politics as not simply a vehicle for power and privilege but as a mechanism for debating public policy, for critiquing and changing the status quo, he or she will be labeled a maverick or a radical. That is only one of the penalties for stepping outside the normal political process.

Perhaps the most blatant, obvious, and pervasive form of behavior modification is advertising. A variety of pressures, signals, and messages that are both subtle and unsubtle are used to persuade us that we should buy things, whether we really need them or not. A whole field of marketing, which employs all the apparatus of psychology and scientific research, is directed toward changing our behavior so that we will select one item over another.

## THEORIES AND TECHNIQUES

Every day we experience attempts to modify the way we act. Not all of them are as dramatic as brainwashing and psychosurgery, but they are no less real. What are the theories behind them, how do they work, and what are their ethical implications?

The most basic definition of behavior modification is Perry London's: getting people to do someone else's bidding.[1] It simply means changing someone's behavior from one form to another, or having that person act the way someone else wants him or her to act. Seymour Halleck, a psychiatrist, suggests that a patient undergoing therapy receives treatment which, to a great extent, is designed to satisfy the wishes of others.[2] Notice the social dimension of this definition. The therapist tries to help the patient to conform to social norms and standards. Neurotic and psychotic people often act in compulsive and bizarre ways that "normal" people consider odd. The patient, if cured, will then act the way mentally and emotionally healthy people do. Whatever the context may be, however, the critical element in behavior modification is a change in an individual's behavior so that he or she will perform an act that someone else desires, or that is considered socially more acceptable.

The techniques employed range from the very simple to the very complex. The very experience of being born into a family and a social environment exposes us, right from birth, to a certain form of behavior modification imposed by family and society. All day we are subjected to stimuli from television and radio, newspapers and magazines, advertising, and even conversation, suggesting that we change from one way of acting to another. Most of these general forms are relatively simple in their strategy and impact.

[1]Perry London, *Behavior Control*, New York: Harper and Row, 1969, p. 4.
[2]Seymour Halleck, "Legal and Ethical Aspects of Behavior Control," in T. A. Shannon, editor, *Bioethics, op. cit.*, pp. 435ff.

Others, however, are more specialized and complex. As outlined by Perry London,[3] they take two basic forms: control by information, and control by coercion.

## CONTROL BY INFORMATION

Control by information, though exercised on the individual by others, aims untimately at helping the patient to achieve self-control. It may take the form of insight therapy, action therapy, or conditioning. *Insight therapy* is the traditional method employed in psychology or psychoanalysis. Here the therapist provides an atmosphere in which the client searches out, through his or her own efforts, the roots of the problem. By discovering the reasons which led to loss of control, a person may be able to achieve a greater degree of control of self and situation. In *action therapy*, on the other hand, the therapist plays a much more active role, deciding on strategies to replace one kind of behavior with another. During treatment the therapist takes charge, so that the client may eventually achieve self-control. *Conditioning* is a classic method of modifying behavior. One is trained to learn to expect a future event by attending to a variety of more or less complicated signals. By attending to these signals and responding to them, a person gradually is able to change behavior patterns. This is the method used in natural childbirth classes. Expectant mothers are taught, with the help of relaxation exercises, not to eliminate the pain connected with labor, but to deal positively with it. This enables them to experience more deeply the joy of giving birth.

## CONTROL BY COERCION

Unlike control by information, control by coercion assigns a much more passive role to the patient. It may take the form of shock treatment, drug therapy, or invasion of the brain by surgery or electrodes.

[3]Perry London, *Behavior Control, op. cit.*, pp. 43ff.

Shock treatment can be administered either through electric current or through insulin. Electroconvulsive therapy sends a mild current into the brain, producing unconsciousness, convulsions, temporary loss of memory, and a feeling of disorientation in time. It can relieve anxieties and bring about a certain amount of control within the person. Insulin shock puts the person in a coma; it has been helpful in the treatment of schizophrenics, or split personalities.

Drug therapy uses tranquilizers, sedatives, anti-depressants, and hallucinogenics to alter the subject's perceptions. Such treatment has produced many dramatic breakthroughs in treating mental illness. Tranquilizers and anti-depressants have allowed many patients to live outside hospitals in their normal environment and to be quite productive in their normal, day-to-day lives. Hallucinogenic drugs, however, when used uncritically, have brought on various kinds of mental illness. This has raised the question whether improvement through drugs is really an improvement over the lack of control that preceded drug use.

The third category of control by coercion is invasion of the brain through psychosurgery or the use of electrodes. There are several forms of brain surgery which are very beneficial in altering behavior and relieving the symptoms of certain forms of mental illness. A major drawback is the fact that such operations are irreversible. The insertion of electrodes into the brain is a less drastic approach. The electrode is controlled by signals transmitted by radio from either the subject or someone else. Such control by electrical stimuli effectively alters behavior and produces various feelings and behaviors. The electrodes protruding from the scalp look unsightly, but otherwise there are no serious problems and no long-term ill-effects.

## ETHICAL PROBLEMS

In making moral judgments about the principles and methods of behavior modification, we must keep three questions in mind: (1) Is informed consent necessary and possible? (2) What happens to personal freedom? (3) What is normal and abnormal, and who decides?

The problem of informed consent to the kinds of therapy we have been describing is particularly acute because, as Dr. Willard Gaylin has pointed out, the very organ that must give consent—the mind—is the organ that is sick. How can we ask an incompetent person to agree to a treatment, especially when that treatment is irreversible, as is the case with psychosurgery? We try to get around this by asking the next of kin or a state-appointed guardian. However, then we have to be sure that the patient is clearly incompetent. Often people who suffer from mental illness are unable to make competent decisions in some matters but are quite competent in respect to others. It gets even more complicated when they make choices that others feel are not in their own best interests. Should we allow people to make decisions which to us appear foolish or unwise? Do such decisions prove that they are incompetent? Who decides?

Closely related to the question of consent is the issue of personal freedom. Are we violating the patient's right of self-determination? This depends on several considerations. Does the illness itself prevent the exercise of freedom? Where there is a choice between competing forms of therapy, is the person free enough to perceive the differences between them and the differences in possible results? This decision-making ability is only part of the whole problem of freedom, but it lies at the very heart of the matter. All forms of behavior modification, after all, aim at giving back to a person a certain amount of control over his or her life. Ironically, in the very process of trying to restore freedom later, we take it away here and now. Is it right to subject a person to the control of others so that he or she may eventually be restored to self-control? Does the end, in this case, justify the means?

The third ethical dilemma concerns the very concept of mental illness. Who is normal, and who is mentally ill? When people act in socially deviant ways, we say they are abnormal, or eccentric, or sick, but sometimes, from another point of view, such behavior can be perceived as normal and healthy. Are health food devotees harmless fanatics or the only truly wise ones among us? It depends on how many harmful ingredients are contained in conventional diets. If a person walks the streets with a sign proclaiming that millions of our neighbors are being secretly murdered, his neighbors say he has "flipped." However, if the streets were in Berlin in 1943, he would be the sanest and best-informed man on the block. This raises a host of social issues. Who has the responsibility to determine what is normal and what is abnormal? If a certain behavior is defined as normal, do we have the right to make everyone conform to that standard, even though some may not want to? The question gets even more sticky in a political context. Are those who dissent from the norms of society or who wish to reform society to be seen as deviant? Are those who are unhappy or dissatisfied with the status quo to be regarded as normal? In the Soviet Union, political dissidents are often not put in jail, lest they be considered martyrs; instead, they are confined to mental institutions. Many feel that this is a flagrant misuse of psychiatry and behavior modification in the interest of maintaining the status quo. Thus the very notions of mental illness and normality are not always as simple and clear as we might think, and they raise important issues of value. In defining what is normal and abnormal, and in applying these definitions to individuals, we must be very clear about the ideologies and interests that motivate us, our government, and our society.

## BEYOND IDEOLOGY

Behavior modification has a negative public image because we usually think of it in ideological terms. Unscrupulous people have used it to gain control of others for their own purposes. Yet this is not the whole story. Mentally retarded and autistic patients have been helped to function and to live productively in society. Prisoners, too, have been rehabilitated, but instances of coercion and excessive use of drugs and other therapies have caused such methods to be largely discontinued.

However, even though it is not always used in a dramatic form, behavior modification does raise the problem of the relationship of individuals to one another and to the society in which they live. Profound value problems and ethical dilemmas are raised when one person tries to influence the behavior of another. When we consider the possible social application of such technologies, the problems are heightened. How can individuals maintain their freedom in the face of social forms of persuasion that are in constant use? How should we deal with deviants from the norm, and how do we establish the norm? Because of the important nature of these issues, behavior modification presents a case study in the relationship of the individual to society and confronts us with questions that still await our answer. What right does society have to make individuals act in ways acceptable to the majority? What right does the individual have to refuse?

## TOPICS FOR DISCUSSION

1. If you are a student, would you describe your experience at this school as one of social indoctrination or as an exercise in social criticism?

2. To what kind of school would you send your children if you had a choice? Why?

3. An Air Force sergeant in Vietnam, in 1966, after over one hundred missions, was hospitalized because he could not deal with fear of flying. Several crews who were well known to him had been lost in action. His condition was diagnosed as Gross Stress Reaction, shown by anxiety, tension, fear of death, and inability to function. After thirty-six days of treatment with psychotherapy and tranquilizers, his problem was

"worked through" and he was able to resume flying within six weeks.

An Air Force publication commented that this case was a fine tribute to the psychiatrists involved. Are any other interpretations possible? Are there any ethical issues implicit in this story?[4]

## RESOURCES

Bandura, A. *Principles of Behavior Modification*. New York: Holt, Rinehart and Winston, 1969.

Birk, Lee, *et al. Behavior Therapy in Psychiatry: A Report of the American Psychiatric Association Task Force on Behavior Therapy*. New York: Jason Aronson, 1974.

Bloch, Sidney, and Peter Reddaway. *Psychiatric Terror: How Psychiatry Is Used To Suppress Dissent*. New York: Basic Books, 1977.

Delgado, Jose M. R. *Physical Control of the Mind: Toward a Psycho-Civilized Society*. New York: Harper and Row, 1969.

Douglas, Jack D., editor. *Deviance and Respectability: The Social Construction of Moral Meanings*. New York: Basic Books, 1970.

Duster, Troy. *The Legislation of Morality: Law, Drugs and Moral Judgment*. New York: The Free Press, 1970.

Gaylin, Willard M., Joe S. Meister, and Robert C. Neville, editors. *Operating on Mind*. New York: Basic Books, 1975.

Halleck, Seymour L. *The Politics of Therapy*. New York: Jason Aronson, 1971.

Lifton, Robert Jay. *Thought Reform in the Psychology of Totalism: A Study of "Brain Washing" in China*. New York: W. W. Norton and Company, 1969.

London, Perry. *Behavior Control*. Second Edition. New York: The New American Library, 1977.

[4]Hastings Center *Report* 6:20 (February 1976).

Mark, Vernon H., and Frank R. Ervin. *Violence and the Brain.* New York: Harper and Row, 1970.

Skinner, B. F. *Beyond Freedom and Dignity.* New York: Alfred A. Knopf, 1971.

Smith, W. Lynn, and Arthur King, editors. *Issues in Brain/Behavior Control.* New York: Spectrum Publications, 1976.

# Chapter Twelve

---

## GENETIC ENGINEERING

The birth of Louise Brown, the "test tube baby," on July 25, 1978, marked the coming of age of genetic engineering. It was the first successful attempt to bring to term a child conceived outside the womb through *in vitro* fertilization. Since that day, future shock is no longer future; it is here, and we have to deal with possibilities and/or dangers for which we are barely prepared and on which there is no public consensus.

On the one hand, there was great joy for the baby's parents, who had been unable to conceive a child in the normal way because of a blockage in the mother's fallopian tubes; and many looked forward to the possibility of children being born to couples who would otherwise be deprived of the chance of being natural parents. On the other hand, there were grave misgivings and second thoughts. Is a laboratory the proper place for a human life to begin? What of the possible abuses and dangers posed by such a process? Public

127

reactions by scientists, doctors, and theologians ranged from enthusiasm through caution to condemnation, and all wondered: Where do we go from here?

In some ways the reactions to the test tube baby birth resembled the intellectual fallout from the first atomic bomb. Until the dawning of the atomic age, most people thought of scientific research and technological development as benevolent forces which helped to solve problems and improve the quality of life. Funding was ungrudgingly provided for scientific research so that new discoveries could be made and progress continued. The money was there, and few questions were asked. However, the discovery, development, and experience of nuclear energy and its many effects brought hesitation and doubt. People realized that nuclear weapons could mean a nuclear holocaust and the destruction of the world as we know it, even of the human species itself. Even the development of nuclear energy for peaceful purposes ran into problems, including the safe design of nuclear power stations and disposal of their waste products. The implications of the development of nuclear power and energy led some to conclude that science, perhaps for the first time, had experienced the reality of sin.

From test tube babies to nuclear energy may seem like a big jump, but the issues are quite clearly connected and can actually throw light on each other. In both instances we are faced with the questions: Should science do all the things it is capable of doing? Or are there limits? And how do you decide?

Even before human life was produced in a laboratory, fast-moving developments in the general area of the life sciences and of genetics in particular had aroused misgivings and raised fundamental questions. Science has moved rather quickly from the discovery of the structure of DNA by Watson and Crick in 1953 to the ability to produce recombinant DNA molecules in the early 1970's. Many feel that we stand on the threshold of being able not only to engineer nature, but also to engineer the engineers according to our designs and purposes. Consequently, some feel that we have gone too far too fast, while others feel that we have not gone far enough and are capable of much more. Both sides agree that we are faced with a tremendous debate about the purpose and goals of science, the development of public policy with respect to science, and the articulation of a variety of value and ethical issues. The latter are challenging and testing many of our most cherished beliefs concerning academic freedom, the value-freedom of science, and the limits of human responsibility.

## THE ETHICAL ISSUES

Genetic engineering refers to the whole process of altering genes, the building blocks of life, in order to produce a radically altered or a completely new individual. As mentioned above, it includes the possibility of the engineer engineering himself or herself. This implies a qualitative difference in the kinds of invasions into human bodies that are now possible. It also implies a significant change in the building blocks of the human being, and not just changes in environment. There is also the problem that these changes may well be irreversible. This situation raises new issues about some old values. We now have to rethink, in a radical way, such ideals and values as freedom, individuality, and privacy.

From this rethinking there emerge three sets of ethical issues. The first concerns the *framework of discussion* within which we operate in this debate, the second involves our *understanding of nature*, and the third concerns the *engineering process* itself.

## THE FRAMEWORK OF DISCUSSION

When we engage in the genetic engineering debate, we are strongly influenced by our fundamental attitude toward science. Four basic attitudes[1] are generally operative, and they should be recognized and evaluated:

1. Science has the right to do whatever is possible.

[1]James Gustafson, "Basic Ethical Issues in the Biomedical Fields," *Soundings* 53:151 (Summer 1970).

2. Science has no right to intervene in the process of life, which is sacred.

3. Science has no right to change the most distinctive human characteristics.

4. Science has the right to foster the growth of valued human characteristics and to remove those which are harmful.

1. *Science has the right to do whatever is possible.* In this view, the only limit placed on scientific research is the limit imposed by technical capacity. New knowledge is valuable in itself, and it does not matter how much knowledge is gained. In fact, the right-to-know is a basic human liberty, so that any restraint is a violation of the investigator's rights. Moreover, it is suggested that intellectual curiosity and growth in knowledge are two of the most distinctive characteristics of the human species, and that to restrict them is to deny our nature. Finally, there is the unspoken assumption that if we have the *capacity* to do something, we may as well assume that we have the *right* to do it.

2. *Science has no right to intervene in the process of life, which is sacred.* The most frequently heard expression of this position is the popular saying: "Scientists shouldn't play God." In its simplest form, it seems to say that we should be passive in the face of nature and natural processes, and ignores the long and accepted tradition of intervening in nature to benefit humankind. Carried to its extreme conclusion, it would reduce us again to hunting and gathering societies, maybe even to starvation. This attitude, however does raise the issue of the mystery of life and reminds us of the elusiveness of nature that confounds even the best-designed experiments. We are urged to look before we leap and to examine seriously our motives and intentions before we act to gain knowledge that we think is critical.

3. *Science has no right to change the most distinctive human characteristics.* This approach insists that there is a limit to what science may do and that this limit is the nature

of the human person as it is presently understood and valued. It assumes that a qualitative difference in human life would occur if the application or research were to change human life as we now know it. It also raises questions about the political context in which science is done. What if these powers to change human nature fall into the hands of those who do not share the values and beliefs of the majority?

4. *Science has the right to foster the growth of valued human characteristics and to remove those which are harmful.* The basic motivation here is to achieve some control over the processes which affect human life and development. The goal is to continue to improve the quality of life. Underlying this position is the conviction that we have an increasing capacity for self-determination and therefore a greater responsibility for what we are and what we shall become.

None of these four theses is found in its pure form. Nonetheless, they suggest a variety of ways in which we can relate to science and scientific capabilities. They help us to think through our expectations of science and to evaluate its possible effects on the course of human development.

## UNDERSTANDING OF NATURE

The second set of ethical issues connected with genetic engineering involves our understanding of nature. Three models[2] of nature are operative in most ethical discussion: (1) power and plasticity; (2) nature as sacred; (3) teleological model.

1. *Power and Plasticity.* In this model, nature is seen as essentially alien and independent of the person, possessing no inherent value and dominated by impersonal forces and causes. It is "plastic" in the sense that humans can use, dominate, and shape it in a variety of ways as they see fit. This model suggests that the person has an unrestricted right to

[2]Daniel Callahan, "Living with the New Biology," *The Center Magazine* 4:4 (July/August 1972).

# THREE MODELS OF NATURE

| Model | Nature | Persons |
|---|---|---|
| Power and Plasticity | alien<br>independent of persons<br>no inherent value<br>dominated by impersonal forces | can use nature as they wish (domination) |
| Nature as Sacred | calls forth reverence and respect<br>created by God<br>expresses its Creator | part of nature<br>entrusted by God with the use of nature<br>responsible for this use (stewardship) |
| Teleology | logic and purpose<br>no Creator as such | can discover knowledge about human life in nature<br>limited in what they can do to nature |

dominate, manipulate, and control nature in any way that can be devised. The only limitation would come from the limits of our knowledge of the workings of nature. In other words, nature can fight back—but only if we are ignorant of how it works. The implication is obvious: we must find out as much as we can in whatever way we can, for knowledge is power.

2. *Nature as sacred.* This model sees nature as a reality to be revered and respected. In its Western religious form, nature is seen as part of God's creation and is rendered sacred by this origin. For the Franciscan theologian Bonaventure, the objects in nature are the footprints or traces of the Creator; through them we can come to know and love God. In the Eastern religious traditions, nature is perceived as an expression of the one cosmic whole of which everything is a manifestation. Humans are to conform to nature, suggests the Taoist tradition, so that they may achieve unity with it and be at peace. The relationship that emerges from these descriptions is one of stewardship. We have been left nature as a sacred trust and are responsible for nourishing it. The person is a part of nature, and if the person is to be respected, so also should nature, which nourishes and sustains all of life.

3. *Teleological model.* This is a secular version of the previous outlook. It sees a purpose and logic in nature, but no guiding hand behind it. In this perspective, it is possible to study nature and to discover its meaning and the significance of human life. This model also suggests that while we may not be bound by nature in any rigid sense, we are at least able to contemplate limitations on unbridled intervention into nature. Thus there are limits to what we can or may do. However, these come not from any externally imposed reality such as God (as in the previous model) but from the inherent meaning of nature itself.

An understanding of these models of nature does not resolve all of the ethical dilemmas involved in human intervention into natural processes, but it does help us to understand where people are coming from when they confront these problems. It illuminates the unspoken premises from which we and others may be arguing, and it provides us with a framework for helping us to evaluate how we may relate to nature and what implications this may have for us both as persons and as a society.

## THE ENGINEERING PROCESS

Ethical issues arise from the genetic engineering process itself when we consider the motives that are operative. The motivation may be either *therapeutic* or *eugenic*.

When the purpose is *therapeutic*, scientists are trying to develop treatments for people who have inherited diseases. In this case the patient has already contracted a disease, and a cure is sought. Genetic engineering offers to help by introducing normal copies of the appropriate gene, obtained biologically or synthesized chemically, into the patient in order to correct the deficiency.

When the motive is *eugenic*, the emphasis is on prevention rather than cure. Some argue that the inheritance of defects and diseases suggests that the human gene pool has deteriorated; hence the need and—in some cases—the obligation to upgrade the quality of the gene pool. This can be done by preventing the birth of individuals who might have some genetic disease or who in some other way could be considered as downgrading the human gene pool.

There are three basic mechanisms for achieving this goal. The first is positive eugenics, the improvement of the genetic stock by selective or preferential breeding. This would ensure that children are born only to parents who have the correct genotype. The second is negative eugenics, the improvement of the genetic stock by preventing the reproduction of defective genes. Thus persons who have genetic diseases or who may be carriers of defective genes would be prohibited from having children. A final mechanism is that of euthenics: modifying the environment to allow genetically abnormal individuals to develop normally and to live relatively normal lives.

This can be accomplished by medical means such as kidney machines or eyeglasses. It can also be achieved socially through hospitals and special school programs to help the handicapped.

These motives are all aimed at dealing with the problem of people inheriting genetic defects, either by curing the persons capable of having children or by prohibiting them from reproducing themselves. This gives rise to many ethical dilemmas. These motivations are attempts to deal with a serious problem and need to be critically examined.

## THE BROADER QUESTIONS

Thus far, we have examined the framework within which genetic engineering can be evaluated, and the motivations associated with it. When we step back from these considerations, we see three broader questions emerging. They concern our growing mastery over nature, our understanding of human nature, and the possibility of limiting scientific research.

1. *Mastery over nature.* There was a time, long ago, when nature was seen as alive and filled with spirits, as a manifestation or emanation of God or the gods. Part of the Judaeo-Christian heritage has been the gradual and thorough "disenchantment" of nature, whereby it has been objectified and desacralized. Humans no longer feel bonds of kinship with nature. Kinship is now seen as historical, looking back to one's ancestors and forward to the future to be experienced by one's children. Left far behind are the totems which signified kinship with certain groups of animals or other relationships to nature. The result has been a growing acceptance and expression of an ethic of mastery over nature.

A key factor in this change of our relation to nature from animism to respectful stewardship to pragmatic dominance has been the process of tremendous acceleration of knowledge. When most people were ignorant of the processes of nature and when areas of knowledge were small enough to allow an individual to comprehend many different disciplines, an ethic of stewardship was bound to be popular; it was the only one available. The limits in human knowledge held in check the more extreme implications of secularization and independence from nature. Now, however, these limits are quickly receding in the face of increased knowledge. It is hard to remain a steward when you can be the master. The emerging new ethic is summarized in the technological imperative: if we can do it, we ought to do it. While this ethic does not totally exclude the attitude of reverence, it does continue the process of objectivication of nature and enhances the possibility of further efforts to manipulate it.

2. *What is human nature?* We would be able to face these problems, and many of the others in this book, if we shared a clear idea of just what it means to be human. The abortion debate has reminded us, in a painful way, that there is little, if any, firm agreement on what we mean by human nature. It's not that we lack for definitions. We have a long list, going back at least to Plato and continuing up to our present crop of philosophers, theologians, psychologists, social scientists, and biologists. They fail to satisfy us, usually because they are so one-sided. Some focus only on capabilities or capacities, others on the potentials of individuals. Some stress the essential qualities of a person, others concentrate on emotions. Still others focus on rationality. Of course, the further problem is that while we don't like any of these definitions individually, we don't like them collectively, either. We are aware of the political and theological context within which these definitions grow, and we know the ideological ends to which they may be put. We tend to be suspicious of definitions, because definitions can be used to serve a particular goal, and we may not like that particular goal.

There is another, somewhat paradoxical reason for the difficulty we experience in defining humanity: our growing scientific knowledge. The more we learn about genetics, the more we appreciate its importance in helping us to define ourselves. The more we learn of psychology and the social sciences, the more we realize that we can be manipulated in a variety of subtle and unsubtle ways so that we might no longer recognize us as ourselves. Consequently, we know that human nature may be much more malleable than we have ever before imagined. Where does that leave us? Some would say that in a time of confusion and uncertainity we should be conservative in defining human nature and should proceed slowly until we know where we're going. Others would conclude just the opposite: that since we are uncertain, we should be liberal and proceed quickly so that we can gain the knowledge we need to help define our nature. Whichever way we go, there is no broad cultural consensus to rely on as we examine the problems raised by human engineering that affect the way we define what a human being is.

3. *Should we limit scientific research?* The very statement of this question makes us uneasy. The repression of ideas has a long and frightful history. People have been destroyed in the name of safeguarding faith and truth. Ideas have been suppressed only to emerge again under the force of their own truthfulness. We know that if we are to avoid that kind of experience we must not make repression a part of social policy. On the other hand, we must also recognize that we are under no moral obligation to pursue any specific form of knowledge. To be sure, there are certain kinds of knowledge we need to survive, but do we need to know everything about everything? Societies may select preferences and assign priorities, but these reflect needs or desires and they may be changed. Is it possible that progress may be an optional goal for society?

There has been a significant shift in the direction that science has taken. Traditionally, its purpose has been to pursue the truth, to understand the laws of nature, and to perceive the relations between the different systems. It operated primarily in a conceptual framework with theoretical models and was preoccupied with discovering the truth of nature. However, there has been a shift, and today science seems bent rather on changing nature and on redesigning it. Scientists speak of modifying nature, of improving it, of helping it adapt to different purposes. If they succeed, nature will be different from what it is now, for we are talking about a series of interventions that have the potential to redesign a future set of events. This change in the purpose of science also changes the quetions we may ask about the limitations of science. Scientific developments, especially those that are perceived to involve high technology and mysterious processes, cause a great deal of fear, and this may prompt the suggestion of some form of limitation.

The major problem here is that science is a public enterprise. The public has, by and large, always approved of science, but people are now beginning to realize that they pay for science with their taxes and that, through government, they set policies and priorities to which science must respond. Thus, future limitations of science may come about in a much different way—through withdrawal of funding, or through regulation to a degree that makes it no longer worthwhile to pursue a particular project. We have to rethink the question of limiting science from the perspective of the relationship between public policy and science policy. The result may be a placing of limits on science, not through a desire to repress ideas or to hide the truths that science might discover, but because of what people think is important. As society perceives its most critical needs, it may realign its priorities and promote other agenda.

## PRACTICAL QUESTIONS

Advances in genetic engineering raise not only broad ethical issues but also practical questions of implementation. Among the most pressing are those concerning *in vitro* fertilization, cloning, genetic screening programs, and the recombinant DNA debate.

1. *In vitro fertilization.* This is the fertilization of an ovum by a sperm outside of the uterus. Since this is most

typically accomplished in a test tube, the first child born as a result of this process has been called a "test tube baby." Such a method allows individuals who are either infertile or have problems connected with fertilization of the ovum to conceive and bear children. Some of the problems associated with test tube births were indicated at the beginning of this chapter. Others center around possible mishaps which may take place. If mistakes are made in the fertilization process, will abortion be accepted as a simple corrective? Would damaged zygotes and fetuses be rejected simply because of the parents' desire for a perfect baby? And where abortion is rejected and a defective child is born, have that child's rights been violated in the very manner of its conception?

There are other problems, too. Surrogates may replace either husband or wife, either from medical necessity or simply for convenience. And even in the absence of such disturbing complications, some question the expenditure of precious medical resources on a process which will benefit relatively few and which, by raising false hopes, may delay or prevent decisions to adopt children. Nevertheless, many feel that the benefits available from this revolutionary breakthrough outweigh even the disadvantages here outlined.

2. *Cloning.* Cloning is a process in which the nucleus from one animal's body cell is inserted into an ovum from which the nucleus has been removed. The result is an embryo that is genetically identical to the donor. This clone will then be placed within a woman's uterus and brought to term. This procedure has the advantage of ensuring the replication of the desirable genotype. Cloning has given rise to science fiction scenarios in which the danger of raising a race of Hitlers or Stalins is foreseen. Such flights of imagination ignore the influence of environment on the gene. Thus while it may be theoretically possible to reproduce an individual who is genetically identical to the donor, it is by no means certain that this individual will have all the same characteristics.

3. *Genetic screening programs.* These programs examine

large numbers of people to acquire genetic information about the individuals in these populations. If they are found to have genetic diseases they can be treated, and if they are carriers of a disease they can make an informed decision about having children. These are obviously desirable benefits. However, certain ethical safeguards must be employed.[3] First, screening programs should have clearly defined and attainable goals; they should not promise more than they can deliver. The subjects who are to be screened should be clearly informed of the purposes and implications of the program and what they can hope to receive from it. Second, privacy must be protected. Information about subjects should not be released without their permission. Finally, their freedom to bear children should not be restricted even though they may run the risk of a genetic disease. Thus, while screening can confer several significant benefits, careful monitoring must be maintained to ensure that people's rights are not violated, even for the best of motives.

4. *The recombinant DNA debate.* The discovery of the process of recombinant DNA, in which strands of DNA are chopped up at various sites, separated, and recombined with other strands of DNA to create a new genetic package, has caused much discussion and debate. If the process can be used to recombine different species, it may be possible to create genuinely new forms of life. This raises several issues. First there is the question of safety. Unless the research facility is secure, some of the viruses or bacteria used in research might escape and be ingested or otherwise become part of the environment. Since no one knows precisely what these bacteria or viruses will do, it is feared that they may pose a threat to people and environment. The second problem concerns allocation of resources. We live in a time of dwindling resources, financial as well as natural. Recombinant DNA is a rather

[3]Marc Lappe *et al.*, "Ethical and Social Issues in Screening for Genetic Disease," in T. A. Shannon, editor, *Bioethics, op. cit.*, pp. 316ff.

expensive process and its practical benefits are not yet determined, so priorities must be established. Society must decide how much to invest in this type of basic research and how much support to give to government and private programs.

A third problem area is the decision-making process. Should decisions be made by scientists, or by a process of government and what criteria should be used? One criterion would be that of *expertise*. Using this norm, a decision to begin or to stop such experimentation would be made on the basis of the relevant facts, a technological assessment, and an environmental impact statement. A second criterion could be *authority*. However, although scientists have the moral authority that comes from competence and expertise, they do not thave the political authority to enforce their judgments on continuing or stopping recombinant experimentation.

A fourth area of debate concerns benefits. Many proponents of such research argue that it could lead to cures for cancer and other diseases as well as increased food production. Others call such projections grossly exaggerated. In this dispute it helps to distinguish general and specific, as well as actual and potential benefits. Better health may indeed result from such research, but it may not be a big enough benefit because of its very generality. Some potential benefits may be very far in the future. Here we need to separate facts from hopes and not sell a research program on the basis of one's hopes but on the basis of what one can realistically project.

Discussions of these kinds are continuing, and there is a possibility of legislation emerging from Congress to regulate the conduct of recombinant DNA experimentation. Meanwhile, guidelines have been developed by the National Institutes of Health. The debate continues, however, and many scientists are expressing dismay at having even brought to public attention the possible dangers that might accompany recombinant experiments. If, in the future, they withhold such information from the public, there may be more problems in store for us.

It is evident that genetic engineering holds many promises but also many threats. In evaluating how this knowledge is to be used and applied, particular attention must be paid to determining who makes decisions as well as the values on which decisions will be based. We must examine the goals of such a program and the uses to which it will be put. While it is important to attempt to improve the quality of life of persons who have various genetic diseases, it is also important to recognize their very humanity and their worth. If such elements are missing from any consideration of genetic engineering, we will create more problems than we solve.

## TOPICS FOR DISCUSSION

1. List the main arguments for and against *in vitro fertilization*. If a class is studying this chapter, conduct a debate on this issue between members of the group.

2. Of the four basic attitudes toward science, which do you find most acceptable? The least acceptable? Why? Compare the choices of the other members of the class.

3. Which of the three models of nature best reflects your own attitudes and values?

4. Describe, in your own words, the human race's journey "from animism to respectful stewardship to pragmatic dominance."

5. The statement that "progress may be an optional goal for society" was unthinkable in most circles even twenty-five years ago. What has made it thinkable for some people today? What is your own reaction to this idea?

## RESOURCES

Beers, Roland F., Jr., and Edward G. Bassett, editors. *Recombinant Molecules: Impact on Science and Society*. New York: Raven Press, 1977.

Dawkins, Richard. *The Selfish Gene*. New York: Oxford University Press, 1976.

Fletcher, John. "Moral and Ethical Problems of Pre-Natal Diagnosis." *Clinical Genetics* 8 (1975), 251-57.

———"Moral Problems in Genetic Counseling." *Pastoral Psychology* 23 (April 1972), 47-60.

Fletcher, Joseph. *The Ethics of Genetic Control: Ending Reproductive Roulette.* New York: Doubleday, 1974.

Francoeur, Robert T. *Utopian Motherhood.* New York: Doubleday, 1970.

Goodfield, June. *Playing God: Genetic Engineering and the Manipulation of Life.* New York: Random House, 1977.

Harris, Maureen, editor. *Early Diagnosis of Human Genetic Defects: Scientific and Ethical Considerations.* Fogarty International Proceedings, #6, 1972.

Hilton, Bruce, *et al.*, editors. *Ethical Issues in Human Genetics.* New York: Planum Publishing Corporation, 1973.

Kass, Leon R. "Babies by Means of Invitro Fertilization: Unethical Experiments on the Unborn?" *New England Journal of Medicine* 285 (November 18, 1971), 1174-79.

Lappe, Marc. "Moral Obligations and the Fallacies of Genetic Control."*Theological Studies* 33 (1972), 411-27.

Ramsey, Paul. *Fabricated Man: The Ethics of Genetic Control.* New Haven: Yale University Press, 1970.

Reilly, Philip. *Genetics, Law and Social Policy.* Cambridge: Harvard University Press, 1977.

Wilson, Edward O. *Sociobiology: The New Synthesis.* Cambridge: Harvard University Press, 1975.

*Assault on Life.* Black and white. 16 mm. 50 minutes. Rent: $35. Sale: $300. Distributor: Time-Life Films, 43 W. 16th St., New York, New York 10011.

*For the Safety of Mankind.* Color. 16 mm. 26 minutes. Rent: $30. Sale: $275. Distributors: Time-Life Films, 43 W. 16th St., New York, New York 10011.

*Chapter Thirteen*

---

# PATIENTS' RIGHTS

A question that has continued to turn up, in one form or another throughout this book, has been: "What are the rights of the patient in this case?" What kind of medical procedures may be legitimately employed in treating the sick? What demands may the patient make? How do we weigh the often competing rights and duties of doctors, patients, and families? These recurring concerns have given rise to a new socio-medical phenomenon—the patients' rights movement.

In some ways this resembles the consumers' rights movement which has had such an impact on business during the past decade. Consumer advocates have focused most of their attention on the quality of manufactured goods, but they have also forced producers to provide information to consumers to help them make prudent purchases. Unit pricing of items in supermarkets and other stores is one result of this movement. Another outcome has been greater truthfulness and accuracy in advertising. The patients' rights movement is not as well defined or as strongly organized, but it is trying to clarify the relations between patients and health-care professionals and to put the rights of patients on a clear and solid basis. Two concrete results of these efforts so far are the patient's bill of rights of the American Hospital Association[1] and the handbook of rights of hospital patients of the American Civil Liberties Union.[2]

## RIGHTS: MORAL AND LEGAL

When we speak of "rights" we must remember that they are sometimes moral, sometimes legal. A moral right, generally, is a claim on some good; it is sometimes, but not always, reinforced by law.

## TWO THEORIES OF RIGHTS

| | |
|---|---|
| • a claim on the community to attain personal goods and the common good | • claims of individuals to goods |
| • means of defining one's relationship to others | • defends individual against society |
| • means of defining duties to others and society | • protects individual's interests against the power of the state |
| • no necessary legal protection of rights | • no corresponding set of duties |
| | • no necessary legal protection of rights |

Ethical thinkers have usually looked at moral rights in one of two ways. In one traditional formulation, they are seen as individuals' claims on the community for those consider-

---

[1]For a copy, see Howard Brody, *Ethical Decisions in Medicine*, Boston: Little, Brown and Company, 1976, Appendix 2.
[2]George Annas, *The Rights of Hospital Patients*, New York: Avon Press, 1975.

ations or conditions which help them to attain personal goods and the common good as well. From this point of view, rights are means of defining one's relationship to other persons and to the community in which one lives. They also entail duties to others and to society; these obligations arise from the fact of membership in the community. Another theory of rights looks upon them as claims of the individual to goods which society may not take away. In this perspective, rights function as defenses of the individual against society; they establish a zone into which the state may not trespass unless the individual grants it the power to do so. Here they do not carry a corresponding set of duties; their function is to protect the individual's interests against the power of the state.

In both these theories of rights, there is no necessary legal protection of the rights of the individual. Thus a person may claim a right to life, but there may be no specific law entitling him or her to that right. Similarly, an individual may have a right to health care, but that does not imply a specific law ensuring a particular type of service—e.g., psychiatric care.

Legal rights, on the other hand, are claims to whose fulfillment I am entitled by law. They are defined, supported, and written into law by the community. They specify, within the framework of the organization of the community, what I am entitled to, which claims may be made on me, and what are the limits of my responsibility. Thus legal rights imply specific obligations or duties which are owed to people or indicate limitations on what may be done to them. For example, competent individuals have the legal right to refuse any form of treatment. Or, to use an example made (in)famous by television police stories, a person arrested and accused of a crime is guaranteed the right to remain silent and to have an attorney present during questioning.

Many of the rights we will discuss are moral but pre-legal—i.e., they are significant claims a person can make on others or on the community, but whose fulfillment is not guaranteed by law. Whether or not these rights ought to be written into law is a separate question. Some moral rights are also legal rights, and these will be indicated.

## THE RIGHTS OF PATIENTS
The patient's bill of rights includes the following:

• *The right to information.* The patient should receive all necessary information concerning diagnosis and treatment in order to be able to give informed consent and to make decisions based on his or her value system. Interestingly enough, the patient's bill of rights states that if it is not medically advisable to give this kind of information to the patient, it should be given to an appropriate person on his or her behalf. Unfortunately, the bill of rights does not indicate what such circumstances would be. It is clear that if a person is comatose or otherwise inaccessible to communication, decisions must be made by the proper proxy. However, it is difficult to understand what medical reasons could be given for not communicating such necessary information to the patient.

• *The right to refuse treatment to the extent permitted by law, and to be informed of the medical consequences of this action.* The right to refuse treatment is a legal right, since any touching without consent constitutes assault and battery under law. It is based on the fundamental concepts of individual liberty and self-determination, which can be secured only if persons can in fact make choices and be in charge of their own destinies. Such liberty, which must involve the right to refuse treatment, has generally been protected by law. The only exceptions are competent adults with dependents, and minors whose parents refuse standard forms of therapy such as blood transfusions for religious reasons. It is also recognized that a refusal of treatment is not of itself a sign of incompetence, and that a mentally ill person is not necessarily, by that fact alone, incompetent. Thus the right to refuse treatment or—in positive terms—to exercise self-determination is receiving strong legal and moral support.

• *The right to privacy.* All case discussions, consultations, examinations and treatments are considered confidential. Persons not connected with the case or not directly involved with his or her care must obtain the patient's permission to be present for such an examination or discussion. This can create problems in a teaching hospital, where medical students and other health-care professionals need to observe examinations and case discussions as part of their training. They also need to perform examinations and procedures even though they are not the patient's physician. The issue here is one of privacy and simple courtesy. These demand that the physician explain to the patient the need to discuss the case with others and, in a teaching hospital, to share information with residents or interns. When presented reasonably to the patients, such permission could be easily obtained and cooperation ensured, while respect for the patient and his or her privacy would be enhanced.

• *Restriction of access to hospital records.* Such records are a necessary part of patient care, for they contain data which document the patient's program and can be used as a basis for future planning. They can also serve as a basis for review of the quality of care, to protect the legal interests of patient, doctor, and hospital, and to provide a data base for research and education. The bill of rights states that the patient has the right to expect that these will be treated as confidential. When they are computerized, however, privacy may be endangered. Will this confidential information be available to unauthorized persons, government agencies, or private companies? The increased use of computers by hospitals presents a growing threat to patients' privacy. Hence patients should be informed of their rights with respect to the confidentiality of medical records so that they can exercise their option, if they wish, to restrict access to such information.

• *The right to know of research and experimentation.* If the hospital proposes to conduct research or experiments which might affect the patient's care or treatment, that person has the right to know and to refuse to participate. This provision is especially important in a teaching hospital where such projects are carried on. It is unlikely that refusal to participate will jeopardize the patient's treatment; moreover, much research simply involves taking blood drawn for one purpose and using it for another, or using part of the biopsy sample for someone's research. Nevertheless, the patient should be informed of this and allowed to make the deicision. At worst, such a regulation will cause a slight inconvenience for the researcher who will have to obtain consent. At best, it will give the patient a chance to participate actively in research's contribution to knowledge, in a manner that will enhance the right of self-determination that all persons possess. It will also serve to remind researchers that patients, though a quasi-captive audience, are in the hospital to be treated for illness and not for the benefit of science. If they wish, in addition, to participate in research, that is well and good, but it cannot, as a policy, be presumed that all patients wish to do this.

Other elements in the bill of rights concern the patient's right to know hospital policies, to receive continuity of care, to have the bill for services explained, and to know what rules of the hospital apply to his or her conduct as a patient. Again, most of this appears to be basic common sense. It is a matter of taking the time to explain to a patient the procedures in effect at the hospital, who is in charge of the patient's care, who the other members of the health-care team are, and how much services will cost. Thus, these elements of the bill of rights neither add nor subtract anything new. They merely specify and make a little clearer the proper relationship between the patient and the hospital. They educate a person in the nuances of this relationship and provide encouragement and confidence for the patient who wishes to question procedures. This will not necessarily create a generation of trouble-makers; it may create people who are aware of their rights and responsibilities and who may thus be in a better position to help in the process of diagnosis, treatment, and therapy. Such an educated patient will be able more accurately to report symptoms and to follow the regimen prescribed.

## AN ANTI-MEDICINE MOVEMENT?

Some may see the patients' rights movement as an attack on the physician or health-care professionals—and in many instances they may be right. There are those who feel that the doctors have too much power and privilege and who will thus use this route as a way of attacking entrenched positions. Such a posture obviously will do little to enhance the quality of the relationship between physician and patient. On the other hand, it has been traditional for patients to place themselves in the hands of the physician and health-care professionals. It was often difficult to obtain information about one's diagnosis or prognosis. Medical records were routinely not discussed or were withheld from the patient. Thus, in terms of power distribution within the relationship, the patient had very little, if any, power.

What the patients' rights movement can accomplish is to enhance the physician-patient relationship by articulating the proper rights and responsibilities of both sides. It does seek to make the patient more active, less afraid to ask questions, and more informed about his or her condition. Such characteristics can initially be threatening to the physician, but in the long run they can also improve the quality of the relationship. If the patient knows that he or she will be treated with respect and will be informed of the salient elements of the diagnosis, treatment, and prognosis in understandable language, then the patient may be less afraid to approach a doctor, more open and accurate in describing symptoms, and more responsive to the prescribed regimen.

The working out of any human relationship is difficult, but especially so when it is between professional and client. The professional typically has skills, experience, knowledge, and expertise which the client does not have; thus the latter cannot evaluate what advice or course of action the professional recommends. To be successful and productive, the relationship must be characterized by trust on the part of the client and integrity on the part of the professional.

However, there is always a power differential regardless of the quality of the relationship. And while power will not necessarily corrupt the relationship or ensure that the professional will needlessly take advantage of the client, nonetheless the client is in the power of the professional. The consumers' rights movement and the patients' rights movement partially address some dimensions of this problem. They attempt to equalize the positions of the two members of the relationship by educating consumers about the products they need and buy, and about the legal rights they have. Such knowledge can give some leverage to consumers.

With reference to health-care and doctor-patient relationship, the patients' rights movement has focused on the elements of informed consent, patient autonomy, and malpractice. Unfortunately, the stress on malpractice has been somewhat exaggerated and has forced some physicians into the posture of practicing defensive medicine; however, the emphasis on informed consent and patient autonomy is well taken. Patients ought to be more active in their own care, and one way to effect this is to inform them of their condition, recognize their autonomy, and provide motivation for them to become actively involved in their treatment. As a result, patients may well become more responsible, more alert, and less apt to drag out the sick-role that keeps them withdrawn from society and from social responsibilities. Thus, while not attempting to replace the physician or to denigrate his or her knowledge and expertise, the patients' rights movement seeks to improve the physician-patient relationship by reasserting that patients should be treated as autonomous individuals with the ability and competence to make critical decisions on their own behalf. In this way the rights and responsibilities of both parties will be enhanced.

While the patients' bill of rights does not specify anything beyond what is minimally present in the law, its value consists in educating patients to begin to appreciate what rights they actually have. If you assume, however, that the bill as presently written defines all the rights a patient has, you are mistaken. Individuals have many more legal and moral rights than are expressed in the bill of rights of the American Hospital Association. In this respect, it is a weak document. It gives the impression that the hospital is *granting* rights to the person instead of simply recognizing rights which already exist. This mistaken notion is offset, however, by the bill's educational value. As patients become more informed about their own rights, and as physicians receive additional experience in law and ethics, the need for such bills of rights will gradually disappear. This will be all to the good, for there is no document that can insure the quality of the physician-patient relationship. On the other hand, such a document may be necessary as the first stage in articulating the kind of relationship that people wish to have with their doctors and with others who provide health care.

## TOPICS FOR DISCUSSION

1. What are some of the reasons that the patients' rights movement has arisen and gained support during recent years?

2. If you were a doctor, would you prefer to have patients who put total, unquestioning trust in you without regard to their own rights and preferences?

3. Do you think the emphasis on patients' rights weakens or strengthens the relationship of trust between them and health care professionals?

4. Do you think the emphasis on patients' rights will improve or lower the quality of health care?

## RESOURCES

Annas, George J. "Medical Remedies and Human Rights." *Human Rights* 2 (Fall 1972), 151-67.

Belski, Marvin S., and Leonard Gross. *How To Choose and Use Your Doctor: The Smart Patient's Way To Live a Longer,*

*Healthier Life.* New York: Arbor House Publishing Company, 1975.

Cassell, Eric J. *The Healer's Art: A New Approach to the Doctor-Patient Relationship.* Philadelphia: J. B. Lippincott Company, 1976.

Etzioni, Amitai. "The Government of Our Body: A Resolution." *Social Policy,* September-October 1973, pp. 46-48.

ſ